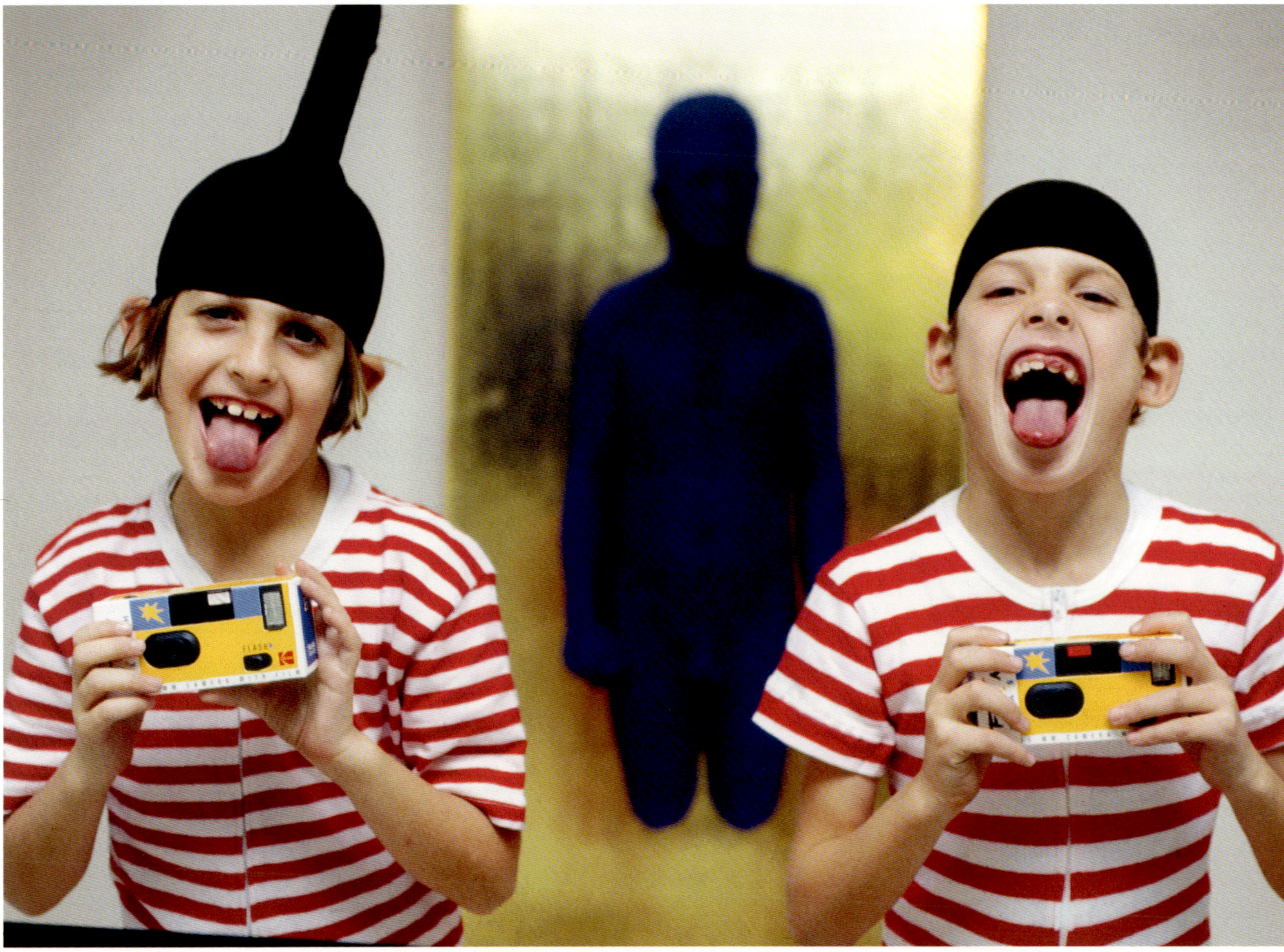

CACHE-CACHE, 1990

←

LES VOLEURS DE COULEURS (PERSONNAGES À RÉACTIVER), 1992

Soon to Disappear (To Pierre Joseph)
Stéphanie Moisdon

Reality takes the form of an insurrection of subjective visions, but there are no riot control police around.
—Pierre Joseph, 2007[1]

1
All quotes are from conversations with the artist and other printed sources.

Pierre Joseph is one of those central figures on the French art scene of the late 1980s whose history is initially linked to that of Dominique Gonzalez-Foerster, Bernard Joisten, and Philippe Parreno, with whom he conceived various visionary projects dealing with shared ideas that have now become significantly popularized: interactivity, real time, duration, the virtual ...

A past history that he has since largely left behind, following a much more solitary and disconcerting road marked by experiments in tracing, displacement, and unfinished mapping, all of which return the artist to his position of wanderer, learner—to his maladjustment.

Pierre Joseph entered contemporary history by the Generation X road, a new category of irresolute individuals aware of the collapse and end of the grand narratives, who wanted to jump off the merry-go-round of status, money, and social climbing that so often frames modern existence. Nirvana's "Smells Like Teen Spirit" (1991) is the obsession and the soul of the "X," at a time when conditions for a new relationship with the world were emerging, marked by the evolution of techno-science, the beginning of the Internet, the end of activism, and the shift from the age of mechanical reproduction to that of access. Inheritors of the intellectual and political nightmare of the 1980s, when businessmen and advertisers were regarded as the modern heroes, this generation eschewed critical thinking in order to have other more underground experiences—those of temporary autonomies, of *Les Voleurs de couleurs* [The Color Thieves, Kodak advertisement, 1987], and the fake pioneers.

Pierre Joseph was to be among the first to bring back to art the weak signs, the low frequencies, and the objects of no value, but also childhood or adolescence as a breach, which engulfed the time of history, of video games, of the disembodiment of toons, and of the "memories of the present"—as he calls his *Personnages à réactiver* [Characters to be reactivated]. To conceive of childhood and adolescence as the source and homeland of art always entails questioning experience and its transmission, experience as a medium and not as a road to knowledge. All the more so when you know how much the expropriation of experience has been implicated in the scheme of modern science. Pierre Joseph acts in a time-frame that relies on the limits of representation—or on its end. That knows that what is most important has not yet been resolved—synthesis, totality, lost and found, execution—and that one must search in the direction of the gaze, of distortion, of surface, of exteriority.

The relevance and singularity of Pierre Joseph's production depends on this beginning, this initial moment of avoidance and obstinate *bricolage*. When the foundations of a new vocabulary of the exhibition, a new way of making art and of being contemporary were being invented. When new playgrounds, real-time movies, and schools freed from productivity were being developed. "A world where 'young' people, those at least who were teenagers by the mid 1980s, had to reinvent the modes of desertion and withdrawal against a profound critical void, to fashion counter-worlds that made it livable—a dissolute world where *to be sad* served in itself as a relationship to the world, and was even the only way to not be utterly unhappy."[2]

2
François Cusset, *La Décennie: le grand cauchemar des années 1980*, La Découverte, Paris 2006.

* * *

"My work is a mapping of my shortcomings. Shortcomings and mistakes are what inform me. It is a way of wandering. A map is a world lost and found again [...] To get lost is to experience tangible de-realization, a moment when everything is floating, without references. It is to visit a world that does not exist, a world whose existence you doubt, but which could exist if you had a map or a notion of it. Then you are no more real than the world you are visiting, lost to yourself, lost to the world.

"I know the map has already been drawn by others; I place myself under this authority and I play with it. Is this a way of re-appropriating knowledge?

"I have been lost in the woods at one time or another, and felt at that moment the sensation that I did not belong to reality anymore. Identical trees all around, whose order escaped me. I did not recognize anything and I did not have a plan (I did not have a strategy).

"You make the assumption that the world no longer exists, left at the checkroom, in order to rediscover it by your own means. To invent a form of opacity for yourself, to rediscover yourself, which is almost the same thing. An attitude of a fake pioneer. Accumulated knowledge, universal like an airbag or capital. In a way, you submit yourself to authority, and you assume that the world has already been thought by others and that you can play with that capital."
—Pierre Joseph, 2003

In the clarity and precision of Pierre Joseph's texts there are all the economy and strength of an observation, of a questioning. They illustrate how, from the standpoints of error and drifting, he never stops pursuing the issues of knowledge and its disappearance, of form and language production, or rather of their uncertainty.

For Pierre Joseph, art is not a personal or collective end in itself, but rather an ultimate futuristic story. For him, neither the world nor art belong to the realm of reality, but rather to that of society's fiction, of anticipatory illusion. An immediate future that is nothing other than the present, and that enables him to produce a "radical exoticism of things" as Victor Segalen put it, that is to say a distance from his own identity—a distance that creates a sort of vertigo in which all kinds of affects and concepts, all kinds of unsolvable and unresolved things, can take place. Pierre Joseph's objects do not have any referents and they could just as well disappear. It is their quality to be unidentified,

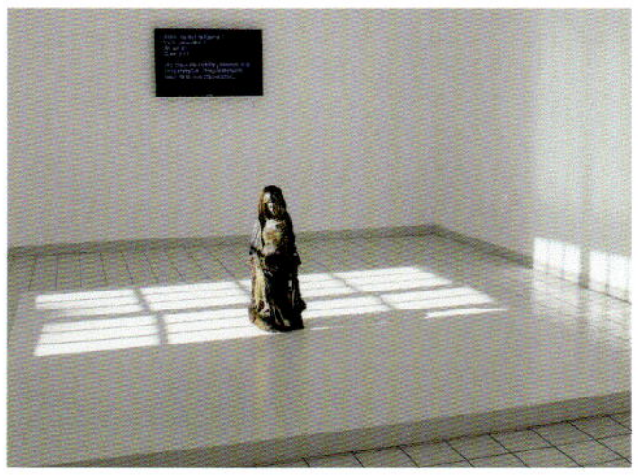

SI CE MONDE VOUS DEPLAÎT, 2006
Exhibition view, FRAC Poitou-Charentes, Angoulême, 2006

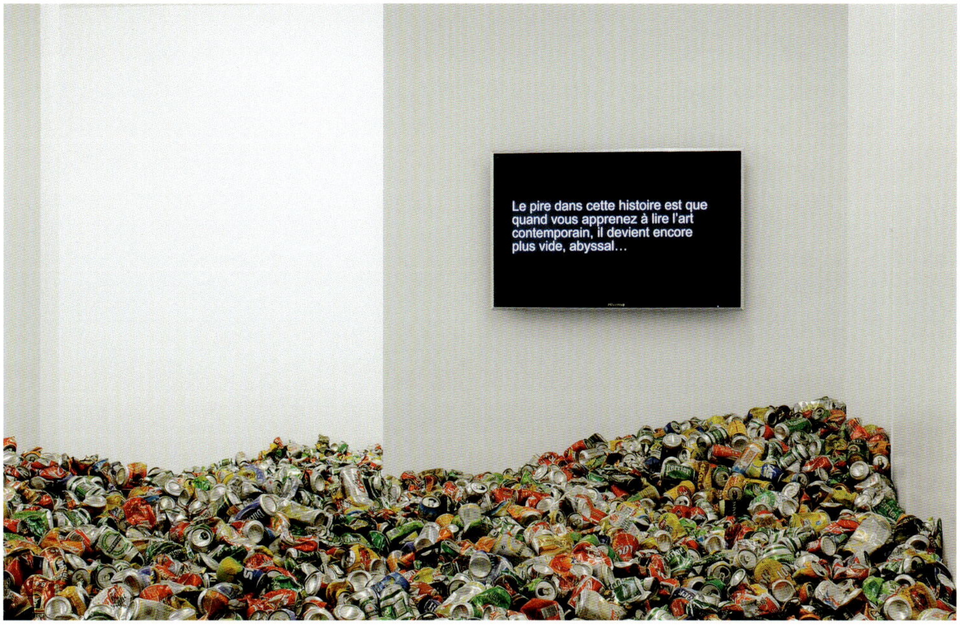

SI CE MONDE VOUS DEPLAÎT, 2006
Exhibition view, FRAC Poitou-Charentes, Angoulême, 2006

indefinite. That is where writing and fiction can convene in a concerted analogy. That is also where clashes occur, antagonism with the context, with symbolic, positive, or functional signification. Pierre Joseph has always had this intuition that in order to create something like a reverse universe or a counter-event, we must absolutely shatter this fullness, this full visibility that we impose on things.

He wonders if, in this virtualized technological world, the dual and indecipherable relationship of seduction would still happen. If art would still happen, if the symbolic form that plays with gravity, the weight of things, and their non-being, would be abolished.

The question of art, of contemporary culture, and of its ruin is at the core of one of his most powerful and most radical works. In his 2006 exhibition at FRAC Poitou-Charentes in Angoulême, entitled *Si ce monde vous déplaît* [If You Dislike this World], Pierre Joseph took a fragment of a text by the American writer Philip K. Dick[3] to serve as a matrix, the beginning of an investigation. The text carries more than an image: a question—that of transmission and possession—which he has been dealing with since the beginning, through the cycling and recycling of the forms of a future almost here, emerging from an invisible point.

In his transposition of Dick's principles of extrapolation, Pierre Joseph took the banal vision of a medieval pietà at whose feet a heap of metal waste, the contemporary flipside of *ugly and ordinary* pity, is emptied out. In doing this, he takes the text not as a prophecy, but as a treaty behind which lies a secret that he has to conquer by force. Pierre Joseph does not expect culture and literature to teach him something; rather they should give him the key, enabling him to get away from the boredom, the repetition, and the orderly spaces of art.
He imagines the spectator as an inhabitant of the Noosphere—a vast network of holographic and informational projections—an inhabitant of the mirror. Neither metaphoric nor poetic, this relates to the biological and political conception of schizoanalysis, a non-category created by Félix Guattari to describe new assemblages, systems of enunciation, and

3
Excerpt from "The Android and the Human" (1972) in Philip K. Dick, *The Shifting Realities of Philip K. Dick: Selected Literary and Philosophical Writings*, Vintage Books, London 1996.

subjectification. “Schizoanalytic subjectivity is established at the junction of the semiotic flows and the mechanical flows, at the crossroads of sensory facts, of material and social facts, and above all, of their transformations resulting from their different assemblage modes. It is the latter that make it lose its character of human territoriality and push it toward both the most primal and most futuristic processes of singularization—becoming an animal, a plant, the cosmos, becoming immature, multivalent sex, becoming intangible ... With this subjectivity, and without completely ceasing to be a thinking reed, man is now adjacent to a reed ‘that thinks for him,’ a mechanical phylum that leads him far beyond his previous possibilities.”[4]

4
Félix Guattari, “Les Schizoanalyses,” *Chimères* no. 1, Bedou, Paris 1987.

In this world in crisis, that we may well dislike, Pierre Joseph puts two conflicting forms from the history of art back in circulation—representations of the sacred and the profane—two markers: “Waste as the archetype of contemporary art and the sacred as what art always ought to be.” To these elements, he adds a third eye, a screen with scrolling fragments of texts and exhibition reviews taken from various blogs. These texts refer back to the unregulated public space of the common observer, to the “discourses of appraisal that form and standardize a certain way of thinking about contemporary art.” Whereas a certain cultural aristocracy collectively wants to improve the morals of the Internet—a garbage can intended to liberate all urges—Pierre Joseph extracts from it other impure and unclassifiable material instead. The idea is that there is always the option of not taking sides, or of choosing the others’ side—the uneducated, the invisible, and the dispossessed.

The montage of these banal statements, sometimes interrupted by flashes of language, is thus loaded with a complexity that subverts the *doxa*. The creed that usually separates criticism from the critical mass, judgment from ethics, expression from impression. What comes out of these bland narratives is a sort of relation, a form of autopsy, a sensation of vacillating: what have we seen before and after us, and if we did not think of it as art, it is still something, so what is it?

We realize what Baudelaire said: that art is the creation of a stereotype, and that what Pierre Joseph has proposed henceforth belongs to everyone. But it can be formulated differently as well. We could say that we now live in this new space, created by him, a virtual reality that was once a production of the mind, an invention of a wild Gnostic species, and that is now the only reality. That we are in his artworks and that the artworks no longer have authors; or they have authors who have not completely disappeared, but have become interchangeable.

* * *

“Personally, I do not save anything.”
—Pierre Joseph, 2006

Must ideas alone be saved, or at least the possibility of a form—of idea as a form—be saved? It is true that in the face of something too accomplished that is an ending, we are reduced to ecstasy and contemplation. In the idea, in the mental space of the idea, the concept must be found again; we must fall short of it or miss it, passing to the other side

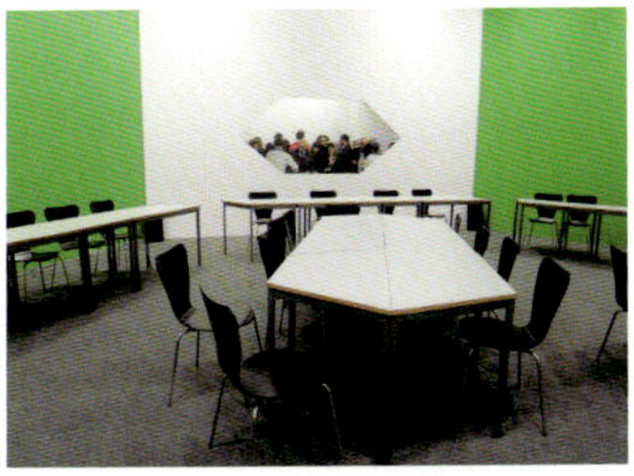

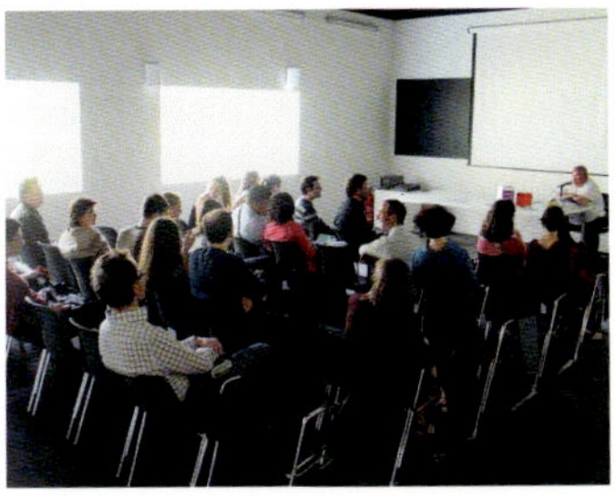

With Stéphanie Moisdon
Scenery for L'ÉCOLE DE STÉPHANIE, Artissima, Lingotto, Turin, 2008
Scenery for L'ÉCOLE DE STÉPHANIE, LA FORCE DE L'ART, Grand Palais, Paris, 2006

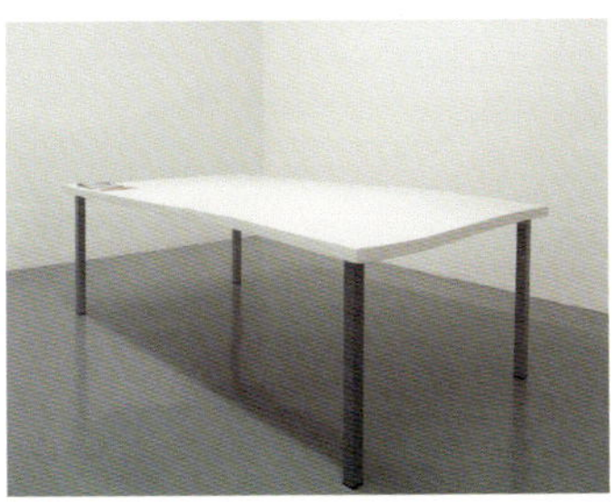

TABLE SANS NOM, 2004

of the screen. The essence of Pierre Joseph's work always lies in destabilizing these too-perfect images, remaining at the base of the thing itself, at the base of the screen. Being unable to clarify things, he remains between two orders of reality: confronting the lost object and anticipating what is waiting for us. For to be radical is to be thus in loss and in anticipation.

Anything Pierre Joseph designates is in opposition to the fact that something should be "real" and could be considered as having meaning, a context, a subject, an object. He knows very well that things have not been like this since the end of modernity, and that even the things that seem simplest always have an enigmatic side to them, which is their radicality. Jean Baudrillard said: "All things are curves." There are no extremities, or all extremities connect in a curved mirror and fulfill their own cycle. All of Pierre Joseph's things are curves. They deny flatness, like *Table sans nom* [Table Without Name, 2004]—a workbench, an indefinable surface, and a scoliotic object playing with its own deformation.

"Could a non-flat table (for instance a surface whose every imperfection intrinsic to its materiality would have been exaggerated) reflect our conceptions in a deformed, warped way as mirrors do with our image at a fair? Could it remind us that our thoughts also are twisted, obscured, as soon as they are magnified, and that our basic knowledge is uncertain like the topography of a smooth surface seen through a magnifying glass? How do you conceive, if nothing is straight around you?"
—Pierre Joseph, 2005

This *Table sans nom* has been through several different exhibitions. The first time it was exhibited autonomously at La Salle de Bains in Lyon in 2004. Then it found another function: it was the teacher's table in the first presentation that I made with Pierre Joseph of *L'École de Stéphanie* [Stéphanie's School] in 2006 in the Triennial *La Force de l'art* [The Force of Art] at the Grand Palais. This displacement, or rather this replacement, aimed precisely to point to a language discrepancy between use and image, taking the distortion inherent to the work itself one step further.

"The surface is not flat, in the manner of bent cardboard. Objects can still be placed on it, but neither their horizontality nor their verticality can be assured. Pens roll [...] Common sense expects a workbench to be as stable and as horizontal as possible; since this obvious fact is called into question, the table becomes an object of reflection."
—Pierre Joseph, 2004

L'École de Stéphanie, a pilot traveling pedagogical project on which we have collaborated three times, is a reflective device in which the lesson is envisaged as a medium, in the same way as sculpture, photography, or video. Each invited teacher, whether they are an artist, a philosopher, a mathematician, a comedian, or a jurist, teaches his or her class once—has one shot—and without any prior rehearsal.

L'École de Stéphanie is a space of projection, of work, of transmission, and of knowledge sharing. A small temporary school, where questions of image, representation, and language circulate freely. A space liberated from rules and authority, grades, and disciplines, running without a program and without manuals. A space inspired by Godard's pedagogy (*France/tour/détour/deux/enfants* [France/Tour/Detour/Two/Children] 1977–1978), by the traces drawn by autistic children recorded by Fernand Deligny, by Célestin Freinet's free school experience, and by all of the other languages that lunatics, idiots, and extraterrestrials teach us. But also, and above all, by the lessons that Pierre Joseph has himself learnt from his various patient attempts: to learn from a children's book in Japanese, from a restorer of artworks, from a boat loftsman, from a factory production line, from a city map, from a final-year high-school student, from a news program, from a snowboard instructor, from chance and what it plots.

The classroom that he created at the Grand Palais is a synthetic image of all classrooms. It is also a virtualized rendition of various 20th-century art episodes. A white screen scrolls down a blackboard; a slit offers a visual opening onto the public space. Films are shown in full light, fading out the pictures' outlines. These references are not an imposition; Pierre Joseph's objects and installations naturally reject scientific mediation and citation. Once again art does not only concern a few owners. In this installation, which materializes the image of a classroom, feelings and sensations that are never taken out of schools are revived: dunces' dreams and first disappointments.

* * *

"As a result of the school format, students are beside themselves, so that they behave as informed subjects and critical observers, but school also produces the works it expects of them: negotiated, shared, situated art objects. Thus it is a question of seeing how, to put it crudely, what we do might have nothing to do with Gilles Deleuze, Alfred Hitchcock, or Bruce Nauman—and our interpretive framework in general—and how something of ourselves might always and finally escape the critical discourse. What do you do with a mermaid, if you don't necessarily want to put her in the 'symbolic' or the 'imaginary' category, and if you keep her, somehow or other, on the edge?"
—Pierre Joseph, 2007

"Perhaps we should evolve without criminal records and without curriculum vitae either. Like routers or gliders. Sooner or later someone else will take it upon themselves to reactivate your proposition of yesteryear, with the ease of ingenuity. To update it. Traces will become immaterial, like spirits, waves that some people will manage to receive. You will not be able to feel guilty any longer because someone will have said to you: 'it has already been done before.'"
—Pierre Joseph, 1996

"It has been done before"—the sentence is familiar. For the 2007 Lyon Biennial, Pierre Joseph distorted its ordinary meaning by means of an untranslatable collective experience of writing and erasing. Being the trickster that he is, Pierre Joseph indirectly answered the question of the current decade—and thus the present time—by means of a strange invitation to a few artists of the French contemporary art scene to re-enact some of his works, retrospectively.

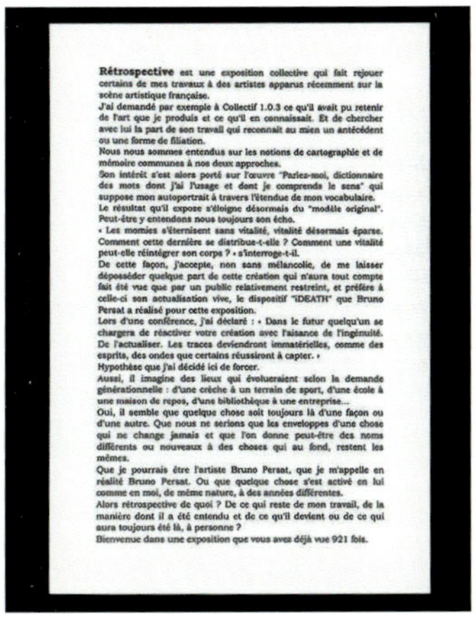

Rétrospective est une exposition collective qui fait rejouer certains de mes travaux à des artistes apparus récemment sur la scène artistique française.
J'ai demandé par exemple à Collectif 1.0.3 ce qu'il avait pu retenir de l'art que je produis et ce qu'il en connaissait. Et de chercher avec lui la part de son travail qui reconnait au mien un antécédent ou une forme de filiation.
Nous nous sommes entendus sur les notions de cartographie et de mémoire communes à nos deux approches.
Son intérêt s'est alors porté sur l'œuvre "Parlez-moi, dictionnaire des mots dont j'ai l'usage et dont je comprends le sens" qui suppose mon autoportrait à travers l'étendue de mon vocabulaire.
Le résultat qu'il expose s'éloigne désormais du "modèle original". Peut-être y entendons nous toujours son écho.
« Les momies s'éternisent sans vitalité, vitalité désormais éparse. Comment cette dernière se distribue-t-elle ? Comment une vitalité peut-elle réintégrer son corps ? » s'interroge-t-il.
De cette façon, j'accepte, non sans mélancolie, de me laisser déposséder quelque part de cette création qui n'aura tout compte fait été vue que par un public relativement restreint, et préfère à celle-ci son actualisation vive, le dispositif "iDEATH" que Bruno Persat a réalisé pour cette exposition.
Lors d'une conférence, j'ai déclaré : « Dans le futur quelqu'un se chargera de réactiver votre création avec l'aisance de l'ingénuité. De l'actualiser. Les traces deviendront immatérielles, comme des esprits, des ondes que certains réussiront à capter. »
Hypothèse que j'ai décidé ici de forcer.
Aussi, il imagine des lieux qui évolueraient selon la demande générationnelle : d'une crèche à un terrain de sport, d'une école à une maison de repos, d'une bibliothèque à une entreprise...
Oui, il semble que quelque chose soit toujours là d'une façon ou d'une autre. Que nous ne serions que les enveloppes d'une chose qui ne change jamais et que l'on donne peut-être des noms différents ou nouveaux à des choses qui au fond, restent les mêmes.
Que je pourrais être l'artiste Bruno Persat, que je m'appelle en réalité Bruno Persat. Ou que quelque chose s'est activé en lui comme en moi, de même nature, à des années différentes.
Alors rétrospective de quoi ? De ce qui reste de mon travail, de la manière dont il a été entendu et de ce qu'il devient ou de ce qui aura toujours été là, à personne ?
Bienvenue dans une exposition que vous avez déjà vue 921 fois.

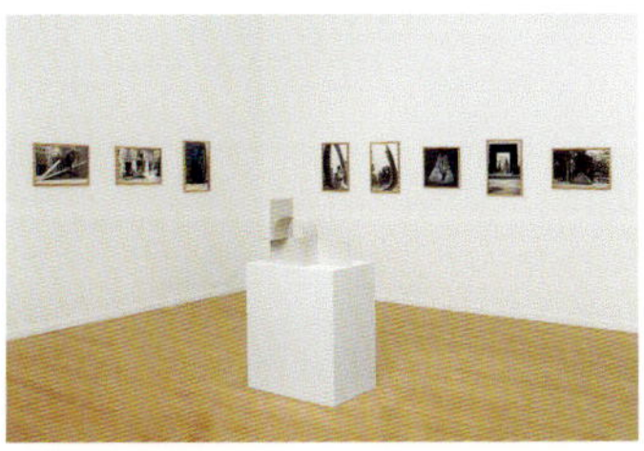

RÉTROSPECTIVE, 2007
Digital label
Exhibition view, 00S. L'HISTOIRE D'UNE DÉCENNIE QUI N'EST PAS ENCORE NOMMÉE, Lyon Contemporary Art Biennial, musée d'Art contemporain, Lyon, 2007
Installation view of Raphaël Zarka's RIDING MODERN ART participation

Rétrospective [Retrospective] was an exhibition based on a theoretical premise: the work in question would have partially disappeared or would only be understandable through what remains: truncated information, commentaries on the Internet, archival fragments. Acknowledging the semi-disappearance of his name and work from institutional and critical circles (for complex reasons due as much to the laws of the market as to his own decision), Pierre Joseph thus produced an instant mirror of this presence-absence status. He addressed a text, intended as a contract and the rules of the game, to Benoît Broisat, Étienne Chambaud, Collectif 1.0.3, Cyprien Gaillard, Mark Geffriaud, Fabien Giraud, Benoît Maire, Bruno Persat, Raphaël Siboni, and Raphaël Zarka. In the exhibition space, the letter takes the form of an animated wall label, programming "something indefinite, a sort of boredom, where things are exhibited indifferently regardless of uniqueness or project types."

The text invariably starts this way: "I asked Raphaël Zarka what he might have retained of the art I produce and what he knows of it, for example. And to look in his work for any part that recognizes a precedent or form of legacy in mine." Whoever the interpreters are, he draws the same conclusion: "the result that he exhibits is a long way from the 'original model.' Perhaps its echo can still be seen in it." A story of expropriation that does not hide its sadness: "In this manner I accept, not without some regret, to be somewhat dispossessed of this creation, which in the end has only been seen by a relatively limited public, and I prefer the live actualization: *le cabinet d'amateur* [the cabinet of curiosities] that Raphaël Zarka has created for this exhibition." "Yes, it seems that something is still there one way or another. That perhaps we are but envelopes for something that never changes and that maybe we give different or new names to things that remain the same after all. That I could be the artist Raphaël Zarka, that my name really is Raphaël Zarka. Or that something of the same nature was triggered within him as in me, many years apart. So, retrospective of what? Of what is left of my work, of the way it has been heard, and of what it is becoming, or of what has always been there, belonging to no one? Welcome to an exhibition you have already seen a 1000 times."

In 2010, Pierre Joseph picked up Jean Baudrillard's text *Pourquoi tout n'a-t-il pas déjà disparu?* [*Why Hasn't Everything Already Disappeared?*], published a few months before the author's death in 2008. Starting from this question: "Why isn't there nothing rather than something?" he animated it with images and developed it on the surface of a digital screen. It makes the time of analog memories and technological desires pass by. In this age of hyper-visibility, of excessive fullness and mastery, in this time of inflated identity, of frantic control of authors' rights and property, Pierre Joseph looked once again toward the future moment when humans as well as artists will invent a specific mode of disappearance, which will have nothing to do with exhaustion, with extinction, with extermination, but with an art of disappearance. In the 19th century Victor Hugo wrote: "The world is only an appearance corrected by a transparency." In the transition to the 21st century, Pierre Joseph has discovered that the transparency of immediacy has taken over all appearances.

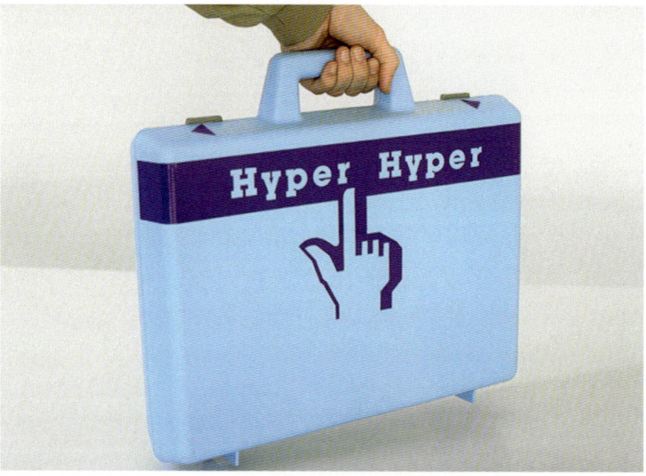

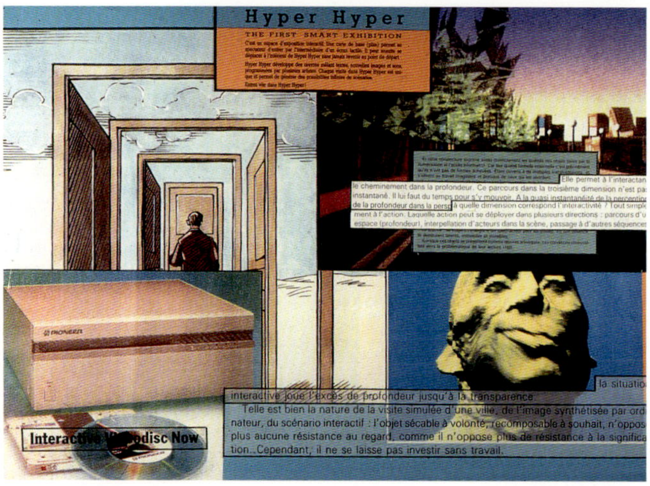

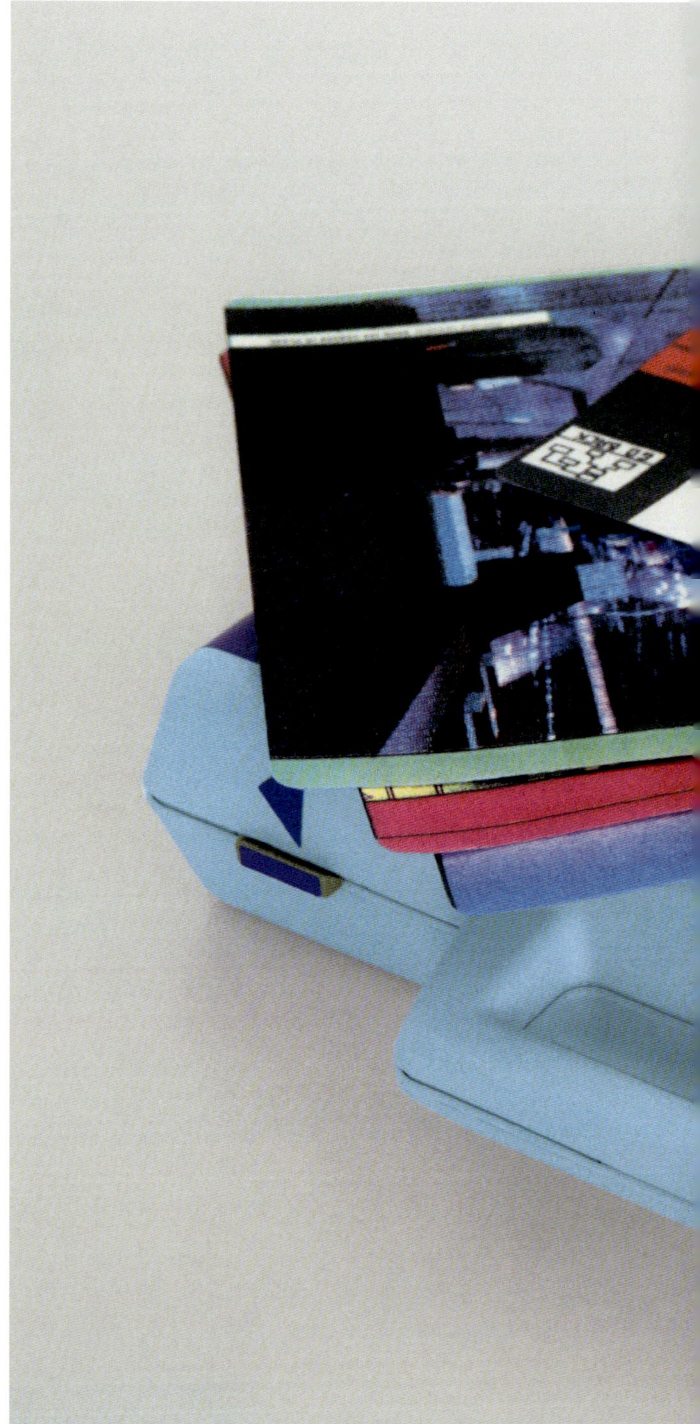

MALLETTE HYPER HYPER, 1988
with Dominique Gonzalez-Foerster, Bernard Joisten, and Philippe Parreno

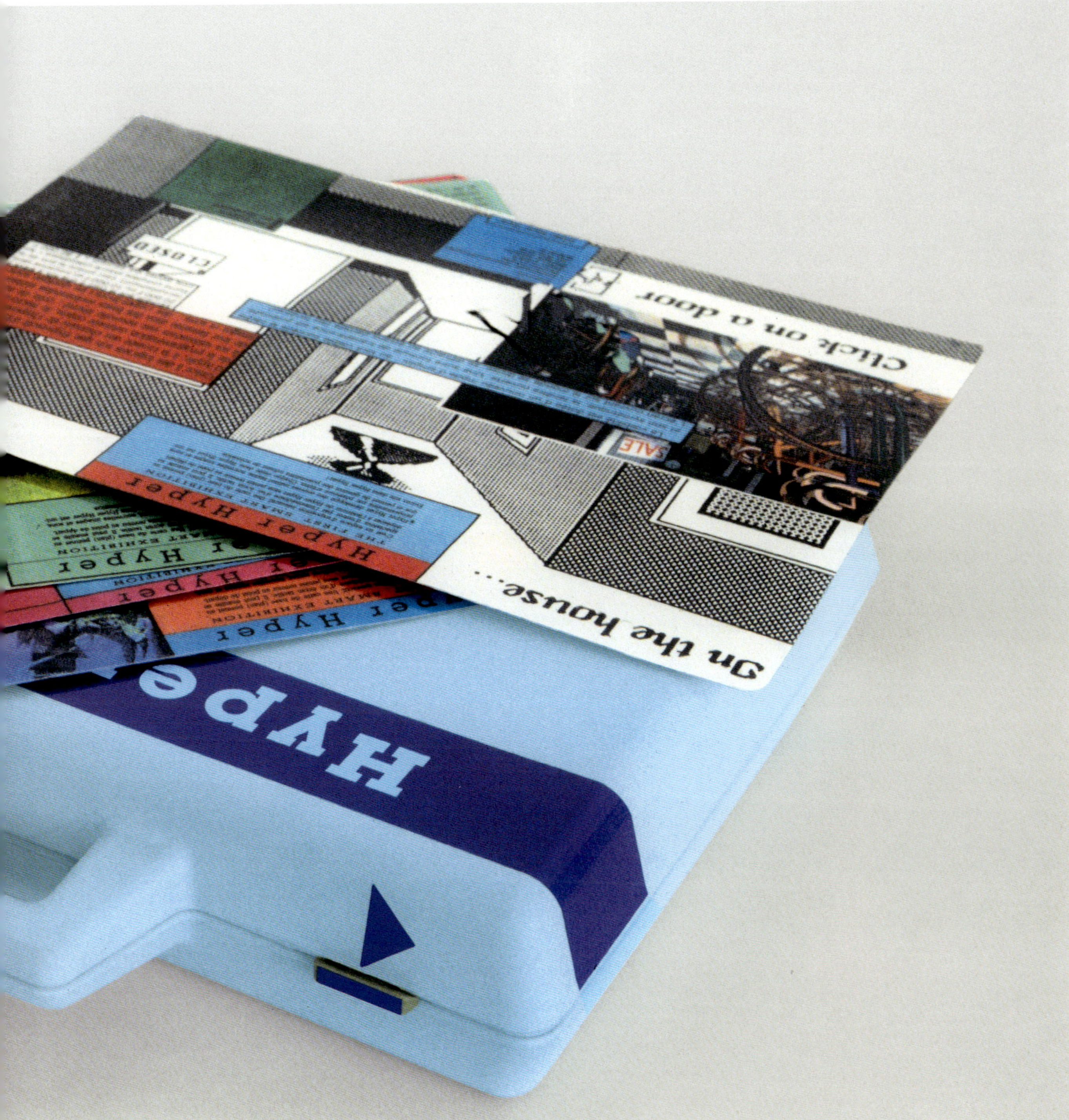
Click on a door
On the house...
Hyper

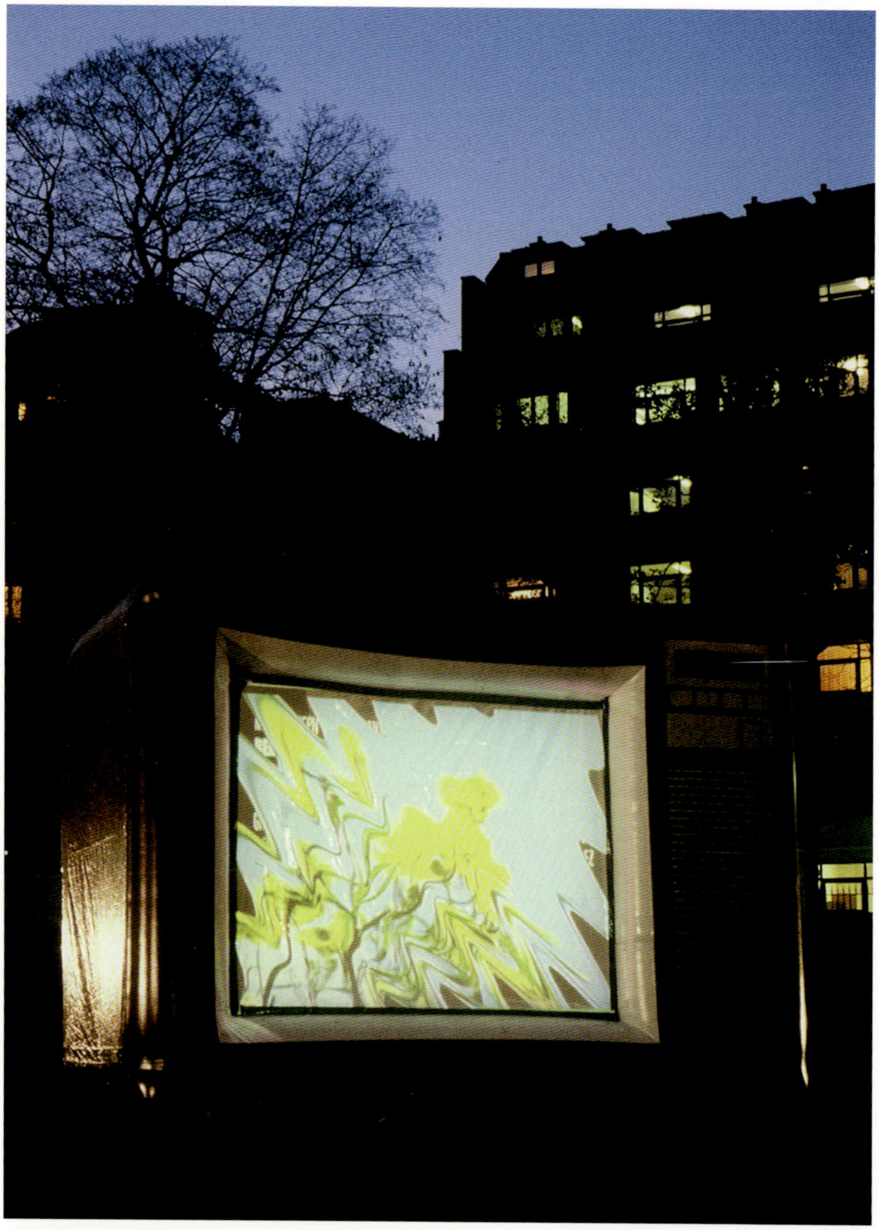

VIDEO OZONE, 1989
with Dominique Gonzalez-Foerster, Bernard Joisten, and Philippe Parreno

OZONE, 1989
Exhibition view, Apac, Nevers, 1989
with Dominique Gonzalez-Foerster, Bernard Joisten, and Philippe Parreno

SAC OZONE, 1988

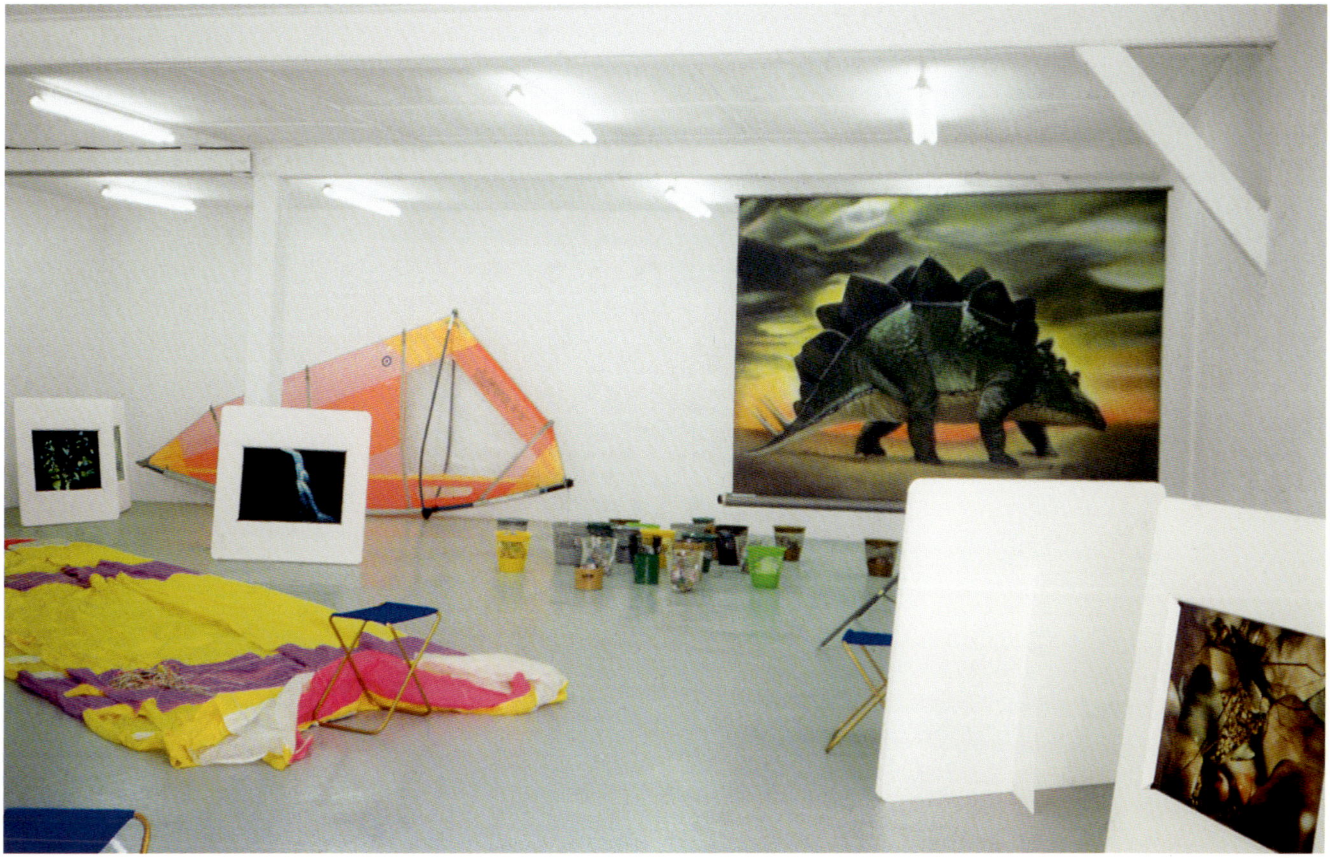

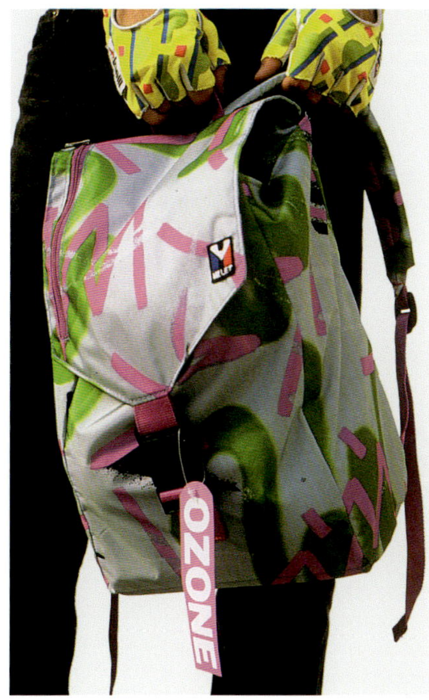
OZONE

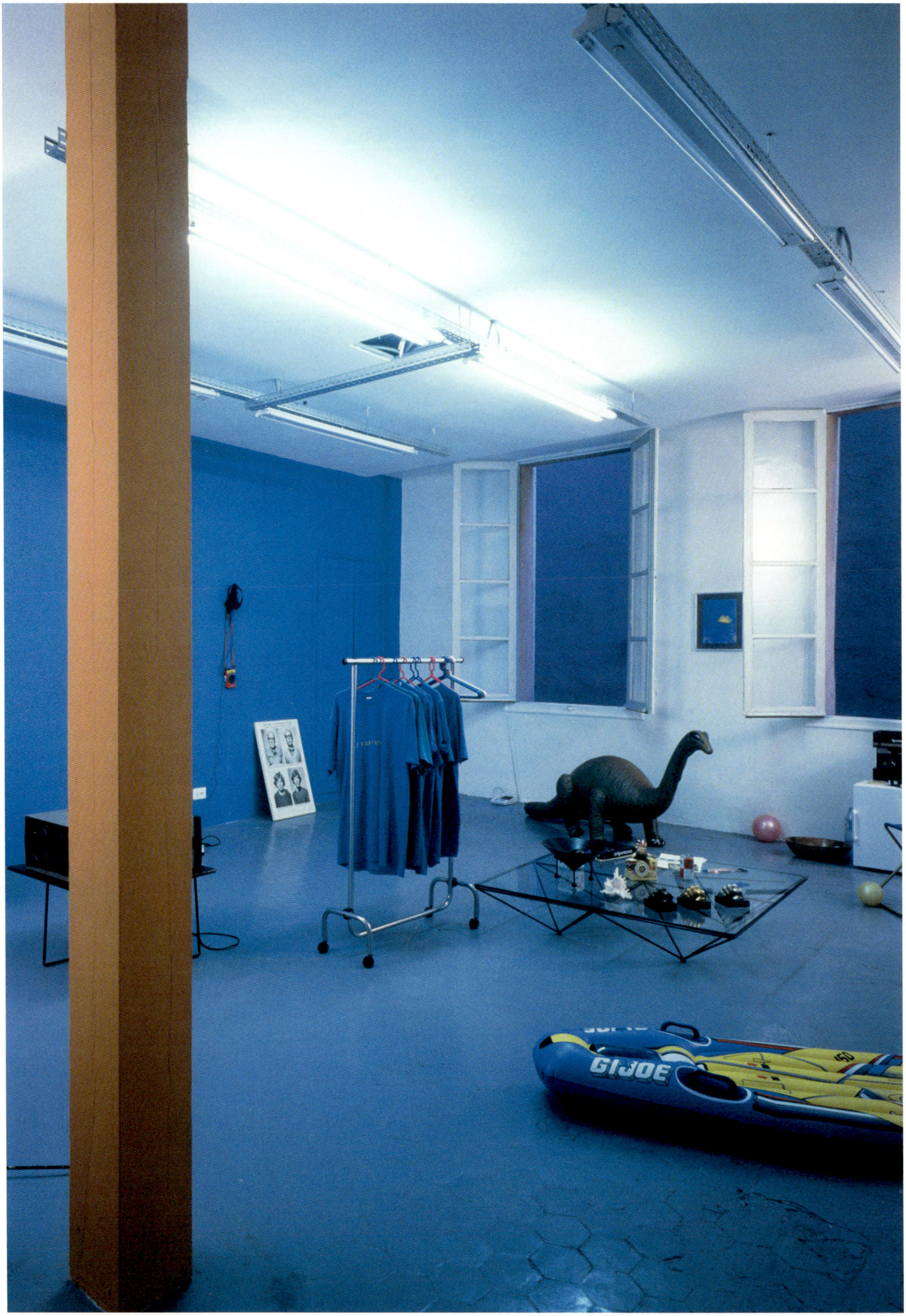
GIJOE

LES ATELIERS DU PARADISE, 1990
Exhibition views and invitation card
with Philippe Parreno and Philippe Perrin

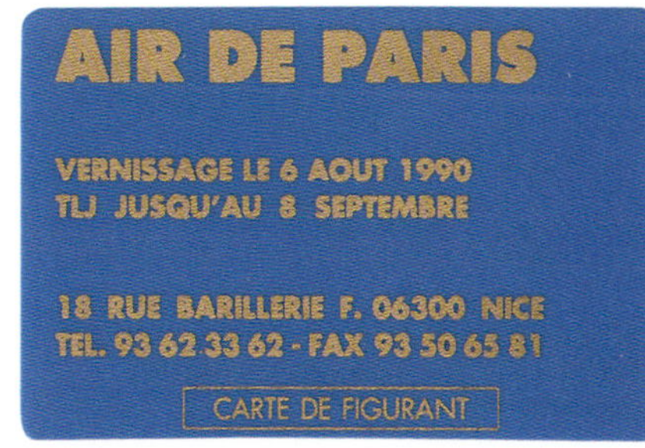

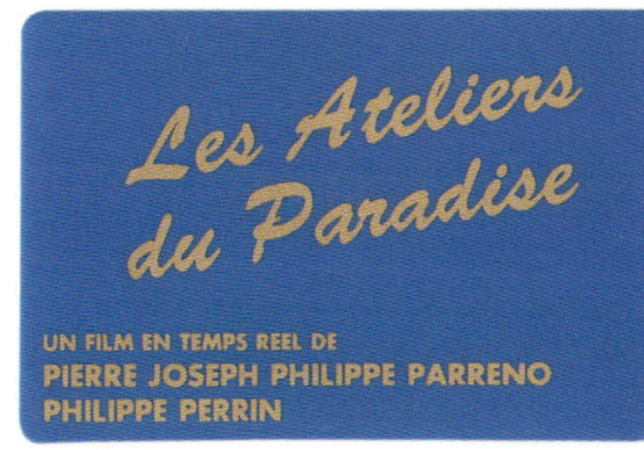

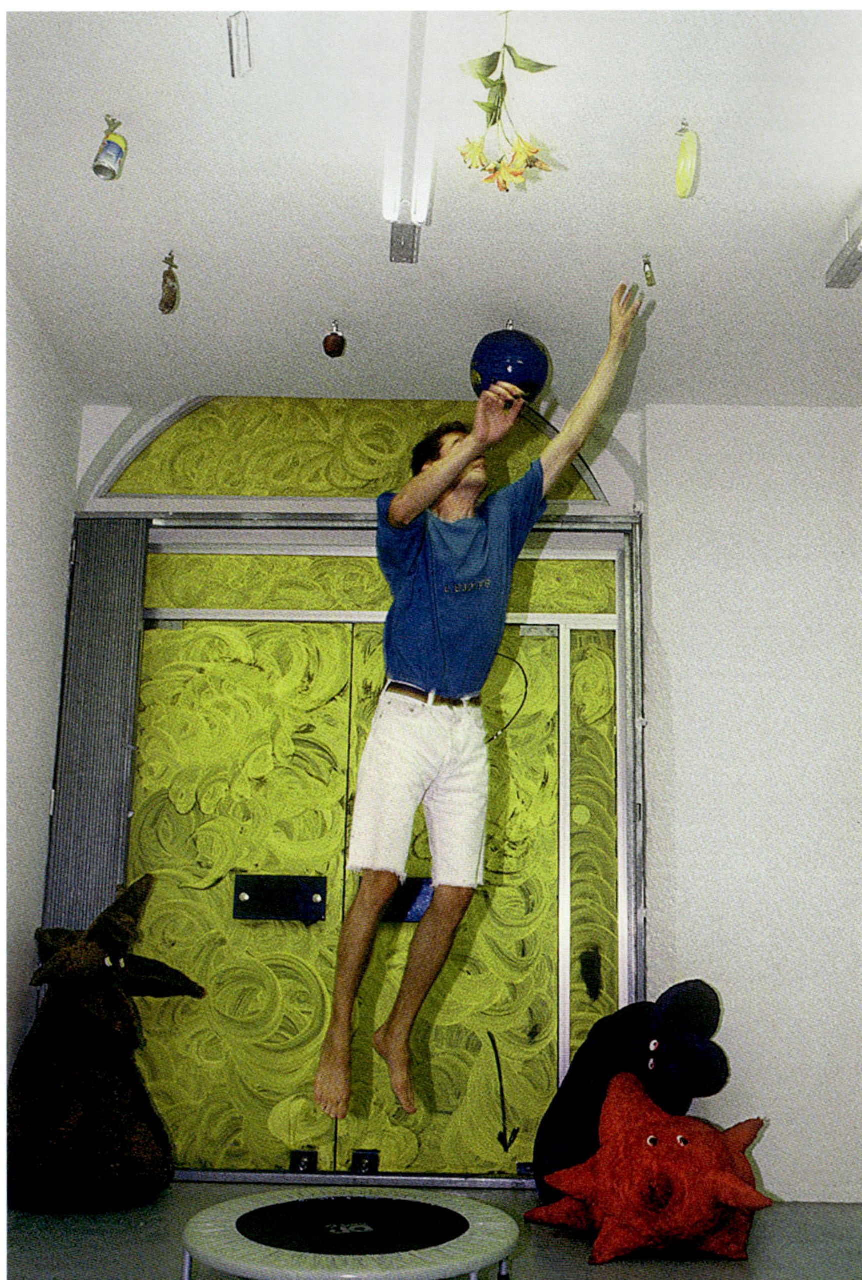

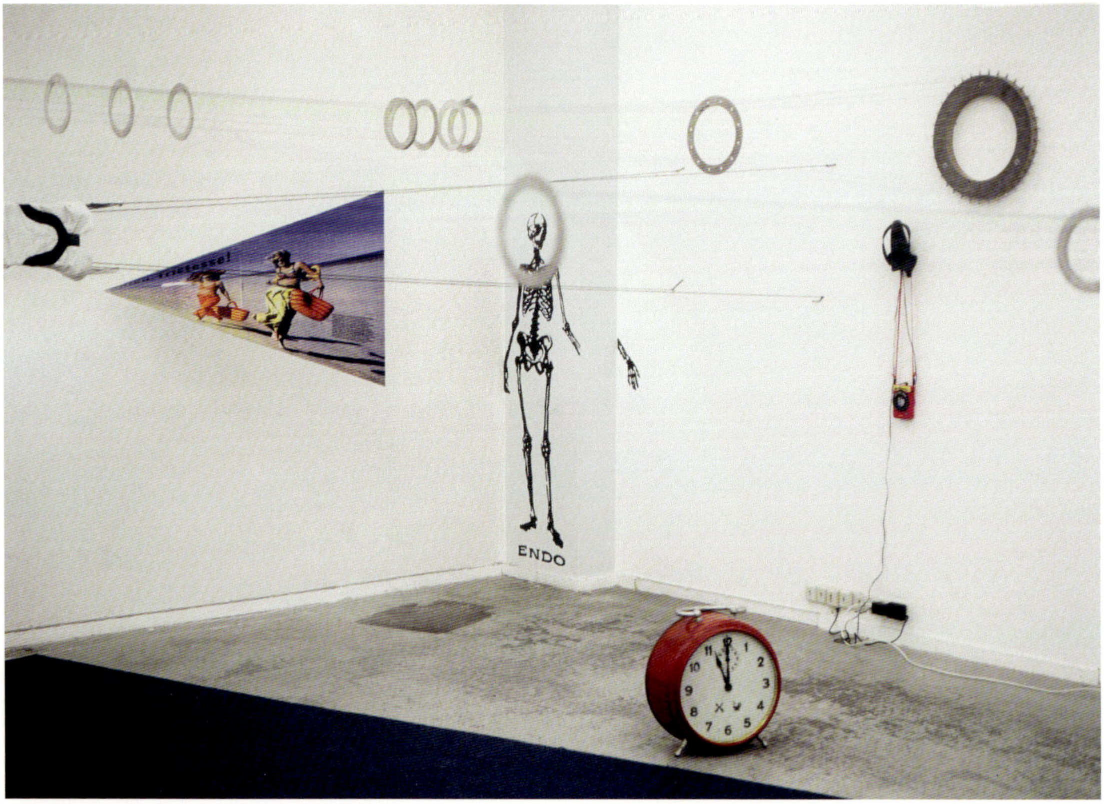

Exhibition view, ONCE UPON A TIME IN CITY BILD, Esther Shipper, Cologne, 1990
with Philippe Parreno

Exhibition view, FRENCH KISS, Halle Sud, Geneva, 1990

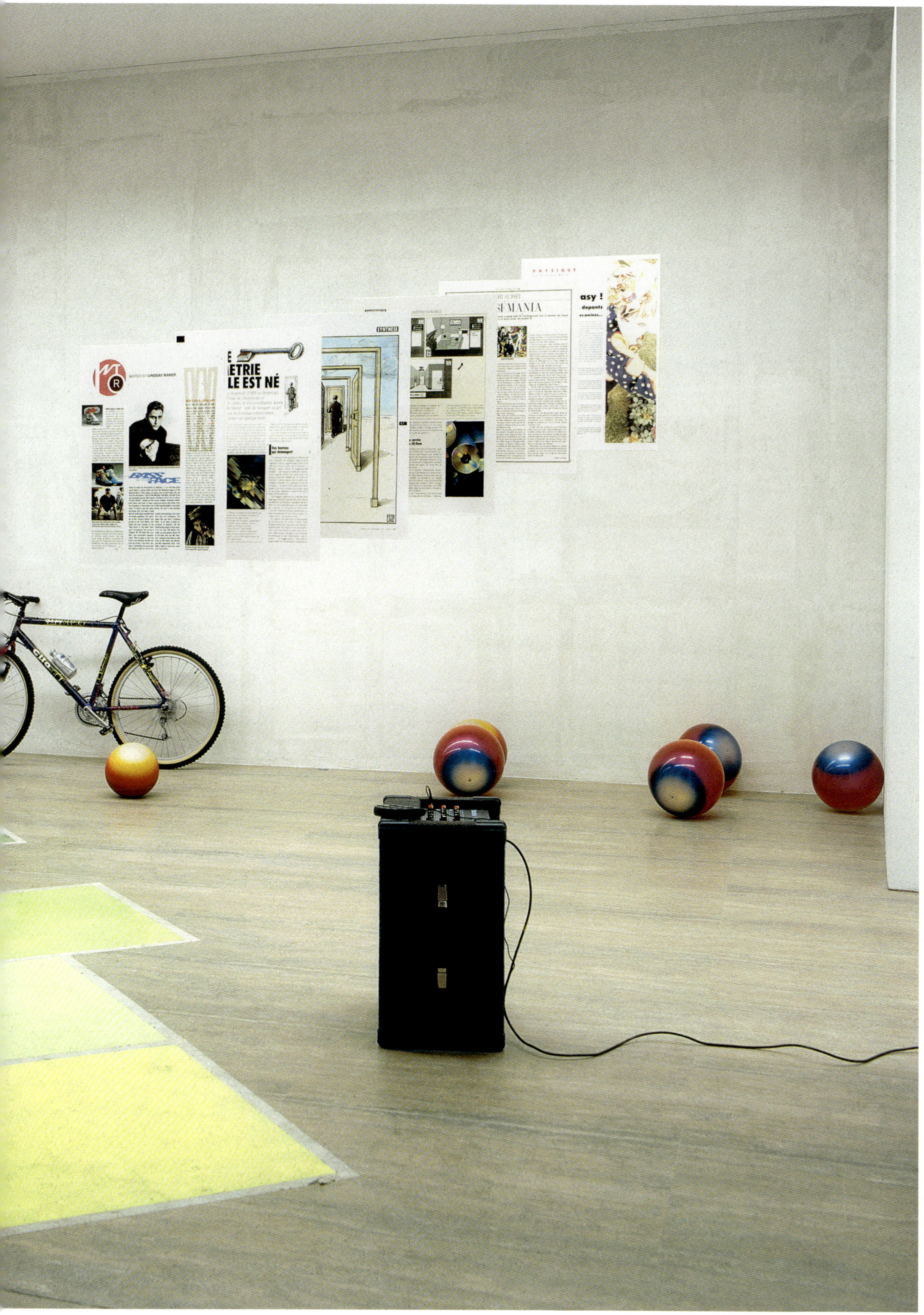

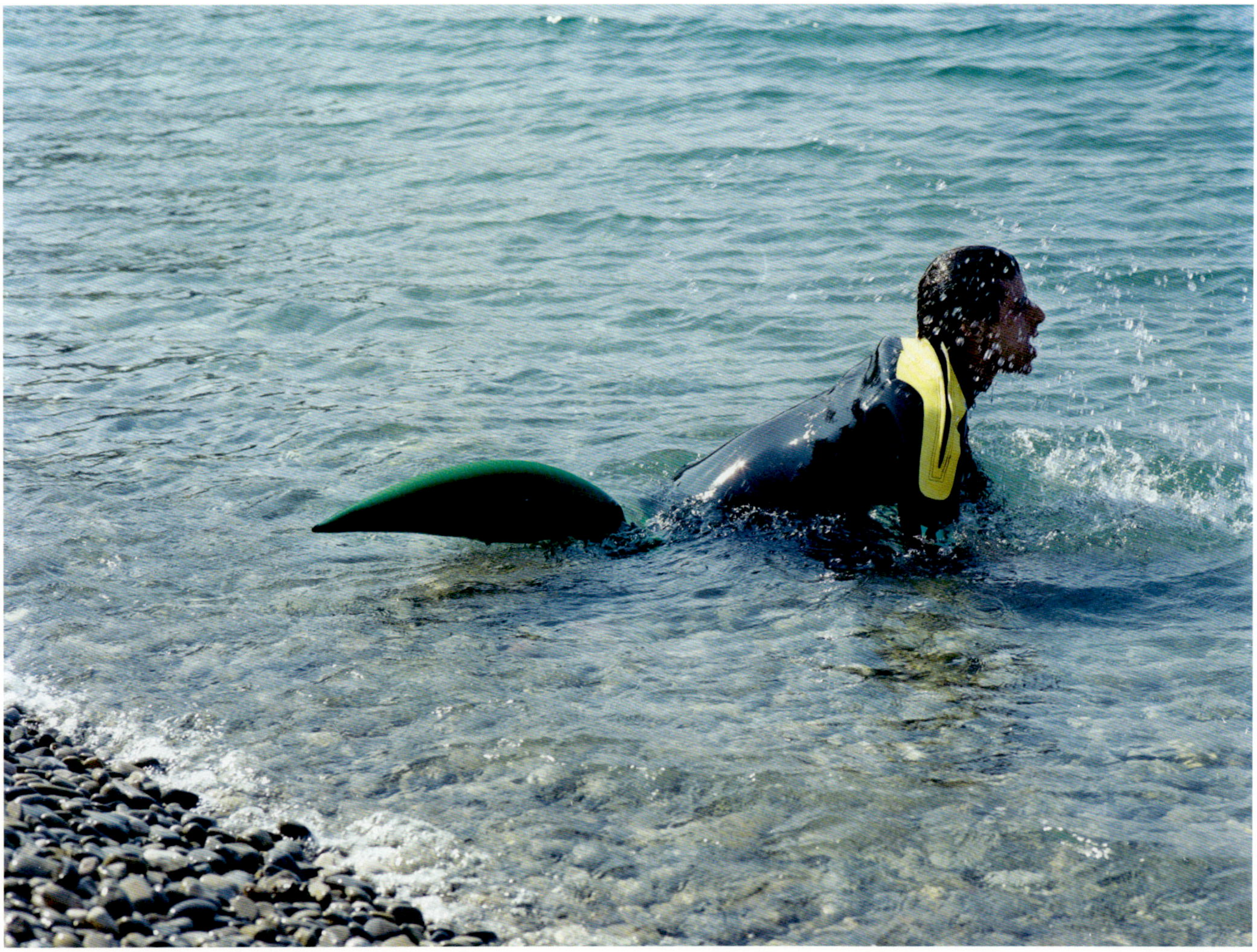

TRY SNAKING, 1991
with Philippe Parreno

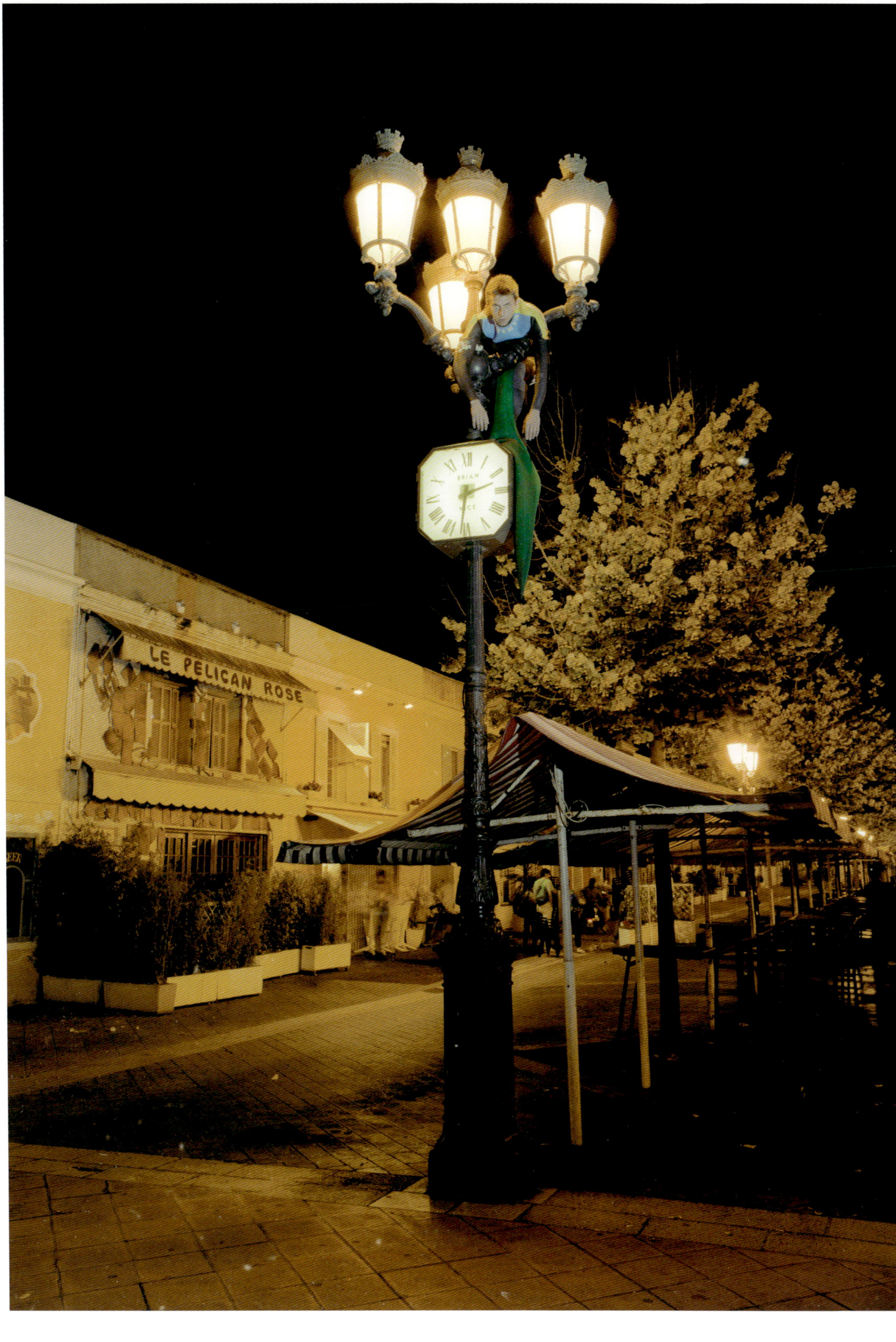
LE PELICAN ROSE

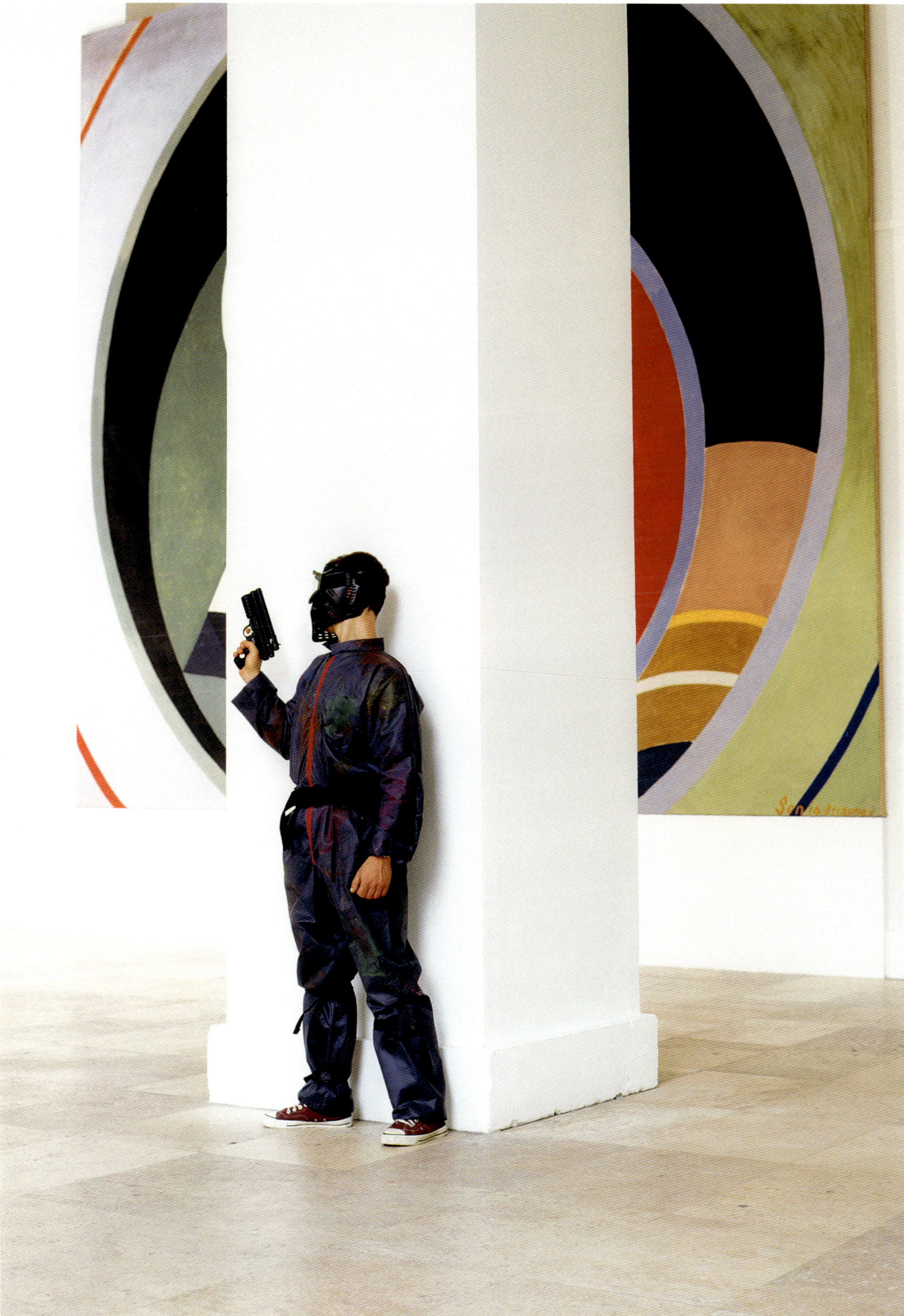

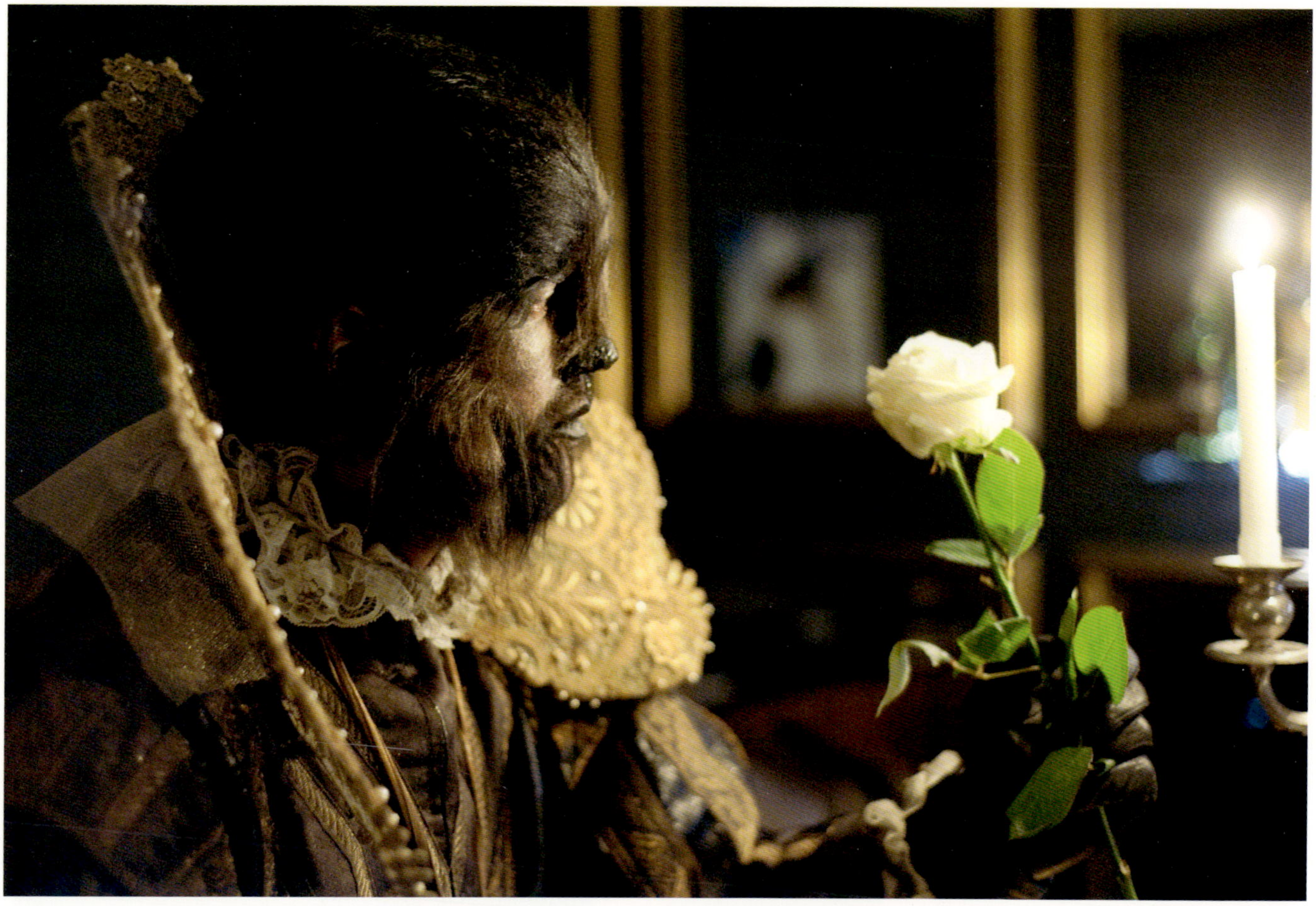

LA BELLE ET LA BÊTE–LA BÊTE (PERSONNAGE À REACTIVER), 1993–2011

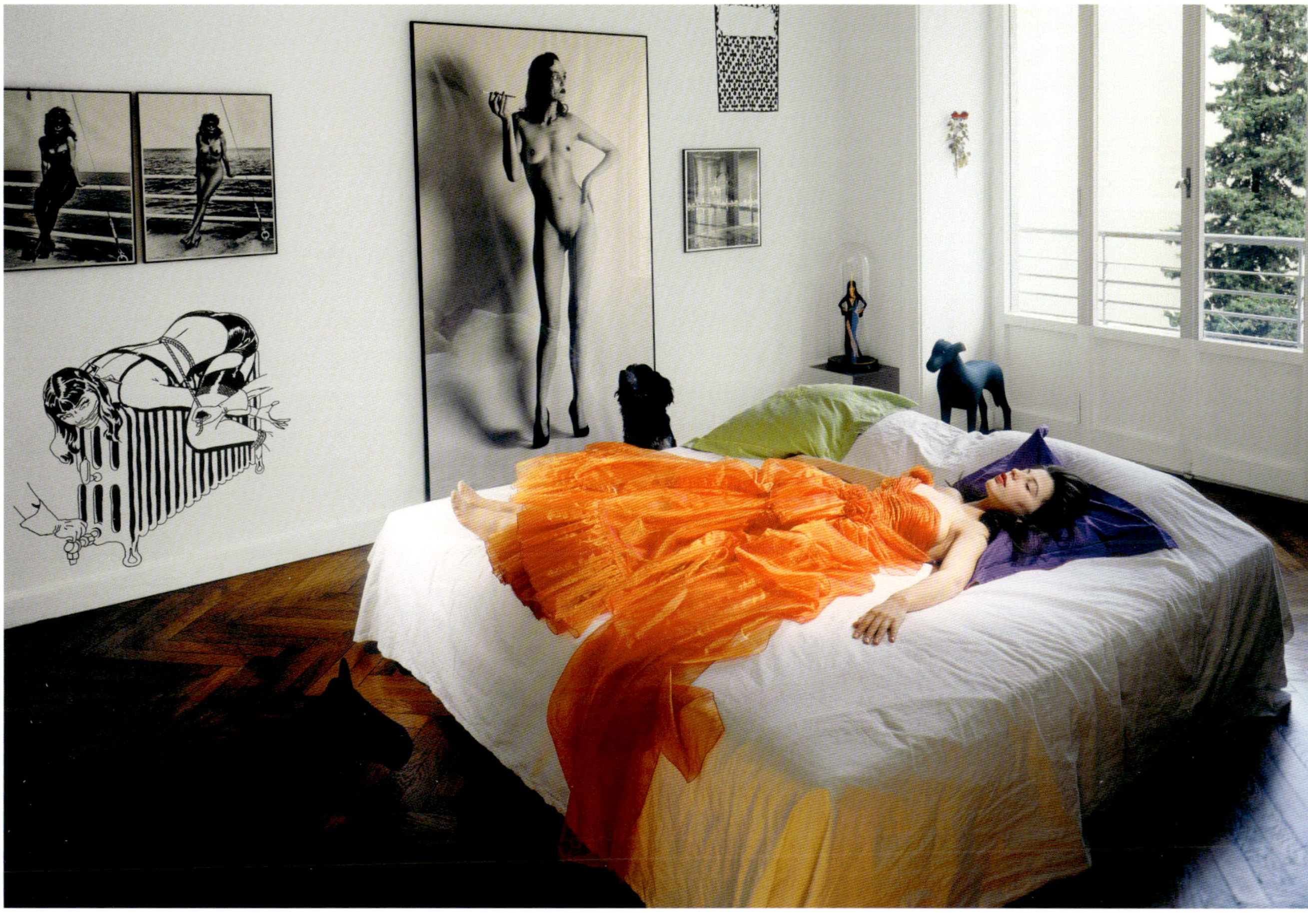

LA BELLE ET LA BÊTE–LA BELLE (PERSONNAGE À REACTIVER), 1992

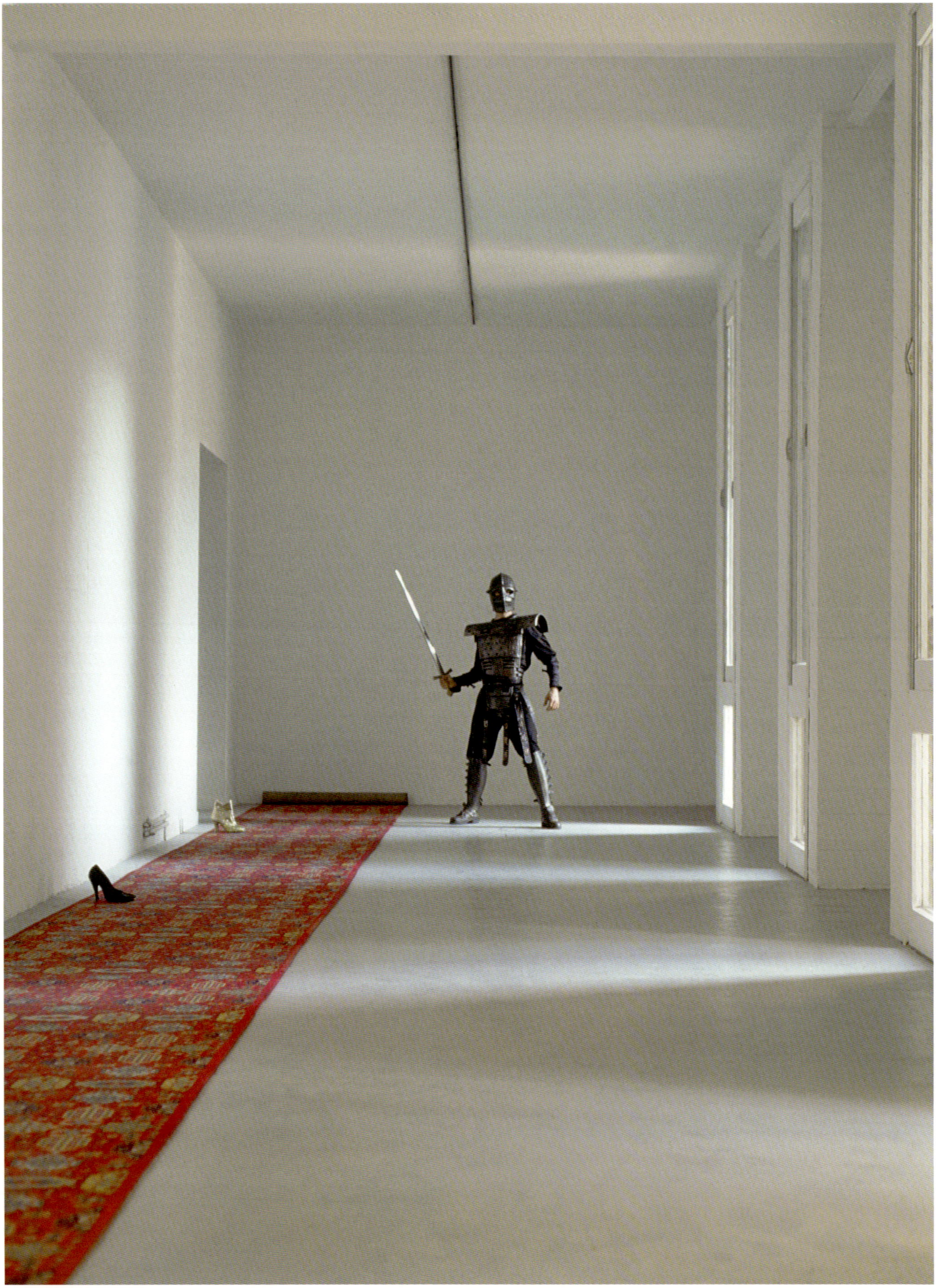

GUERRIER MÉDIÉVAL (PERSONNAGE À RÉACTIVER), 1991

ART, LA FÉE (PERSONNAGE À RÉACTIVER), 1992

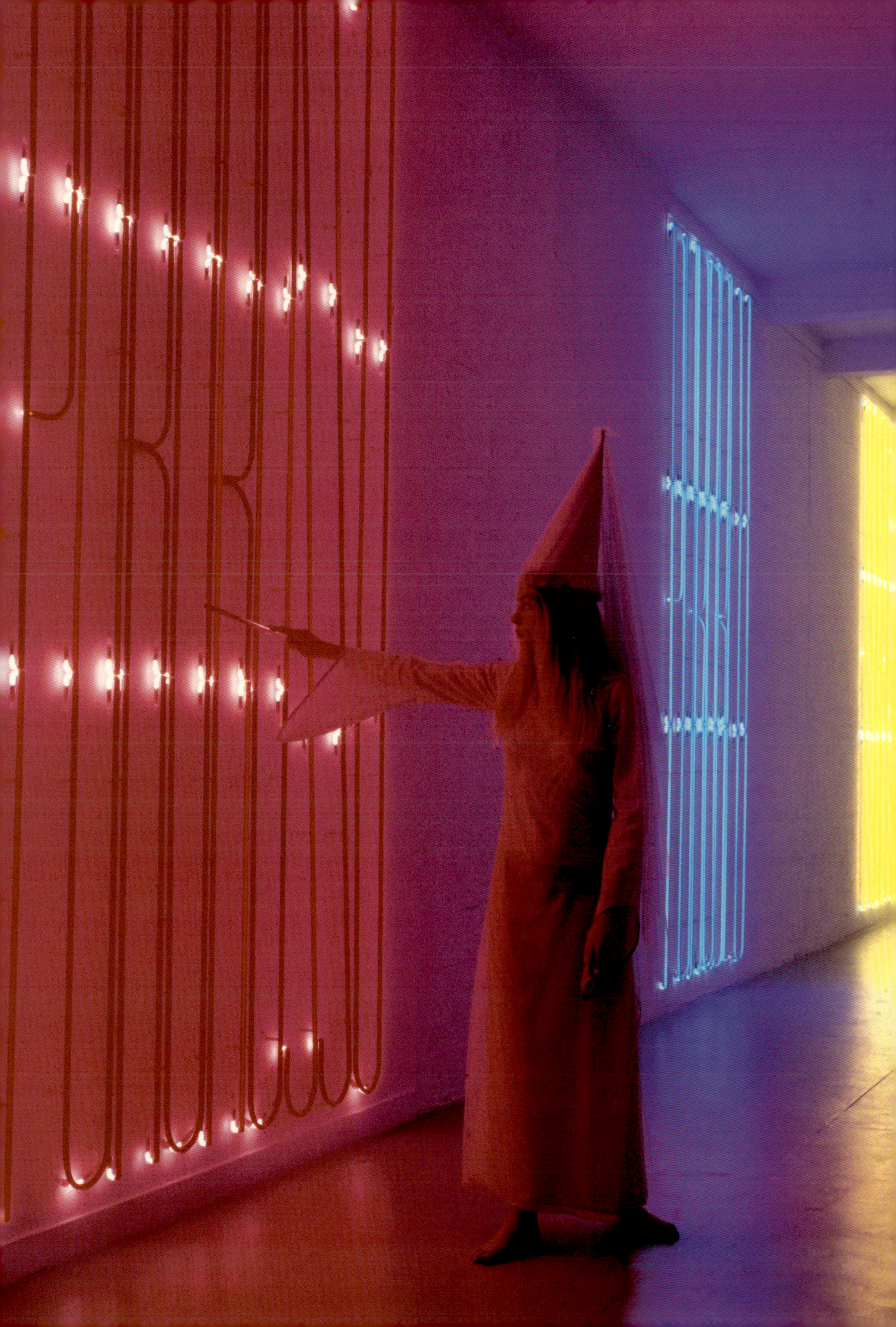

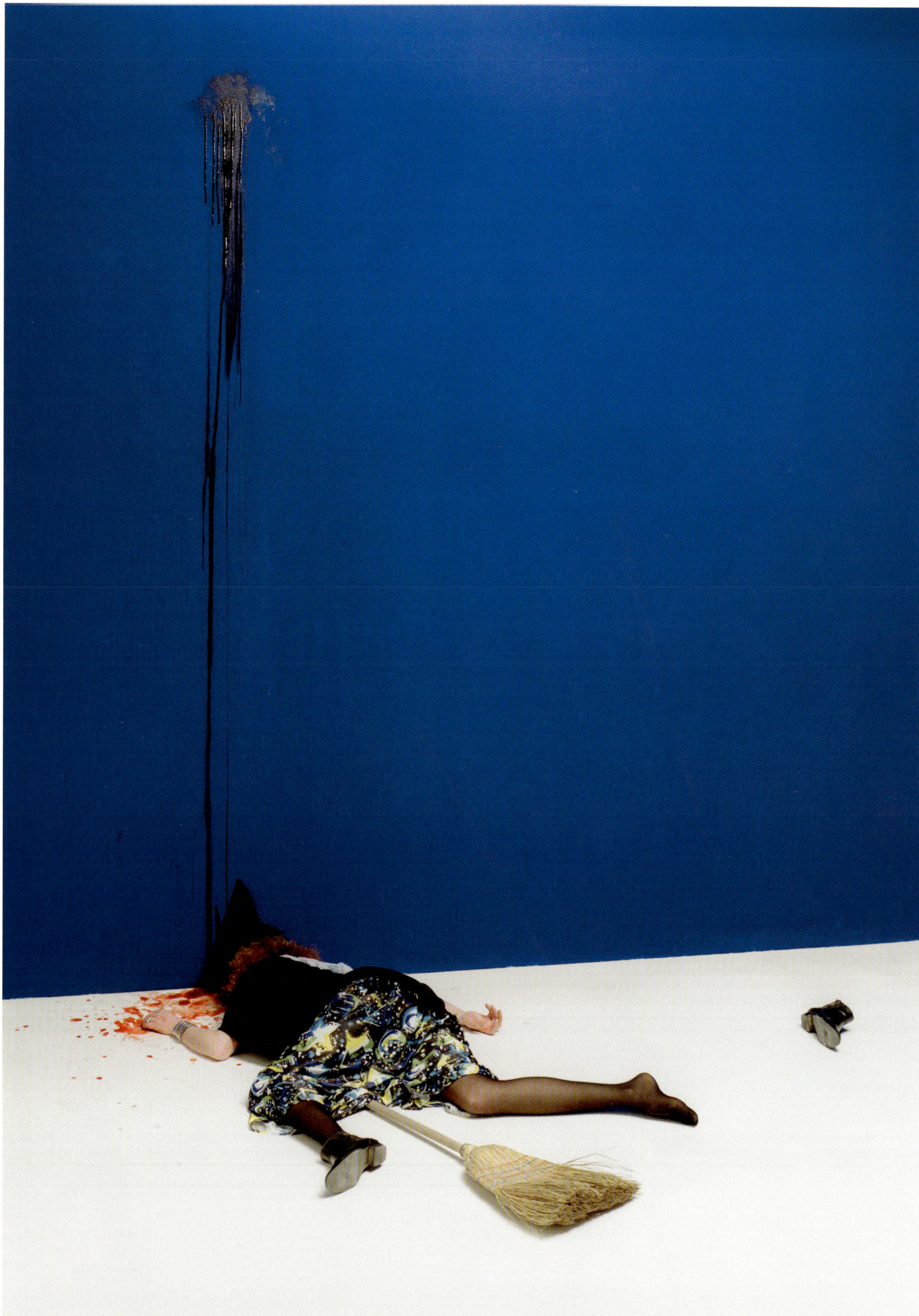

LE GRAND BLEU (TRIPTYQUE): LA SORCIÈRE (PERSONNAGE À RÉACTIVER), 1993

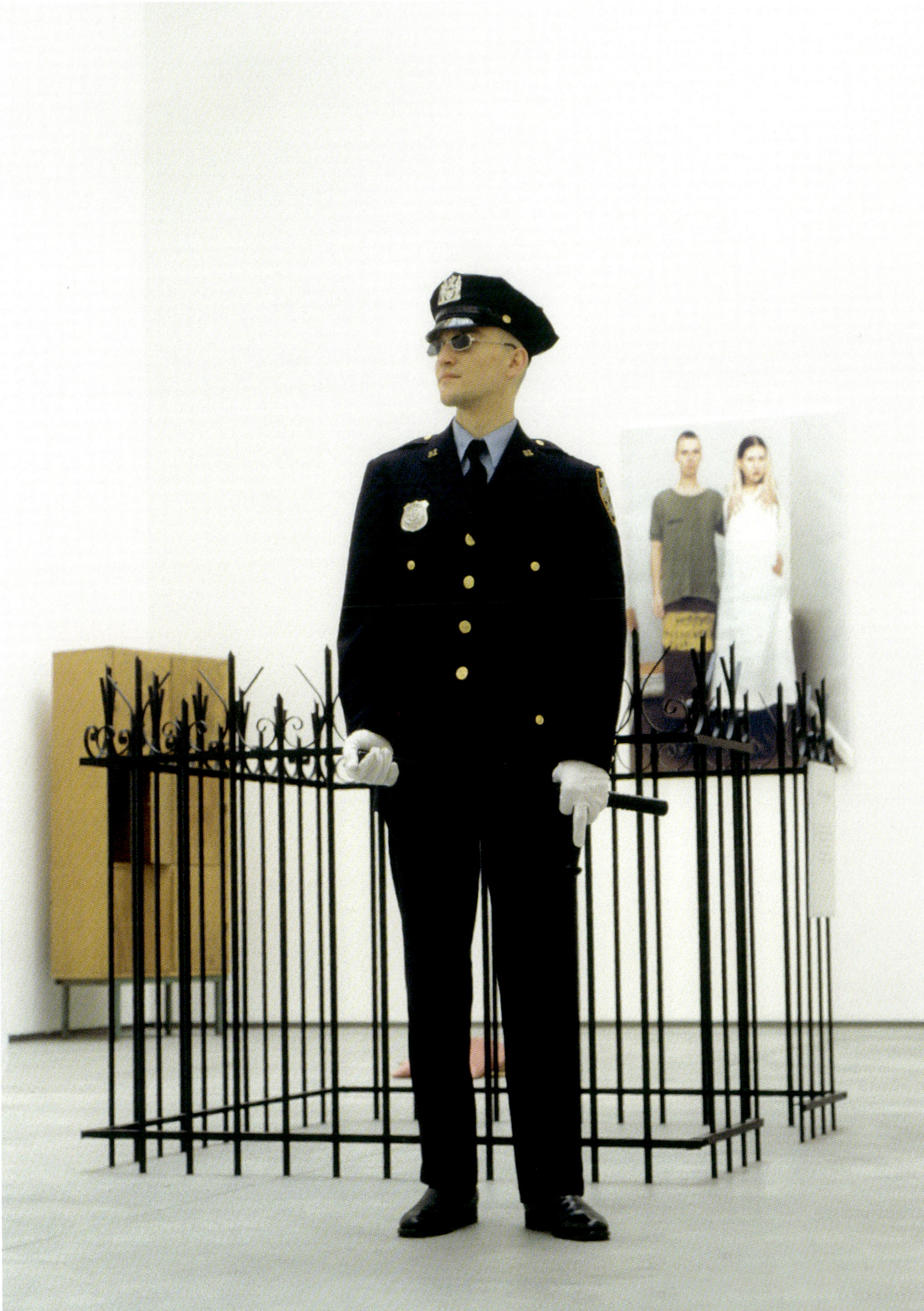

LE POLICIER (PERSONNAGE À RÉACTIVER), 1993

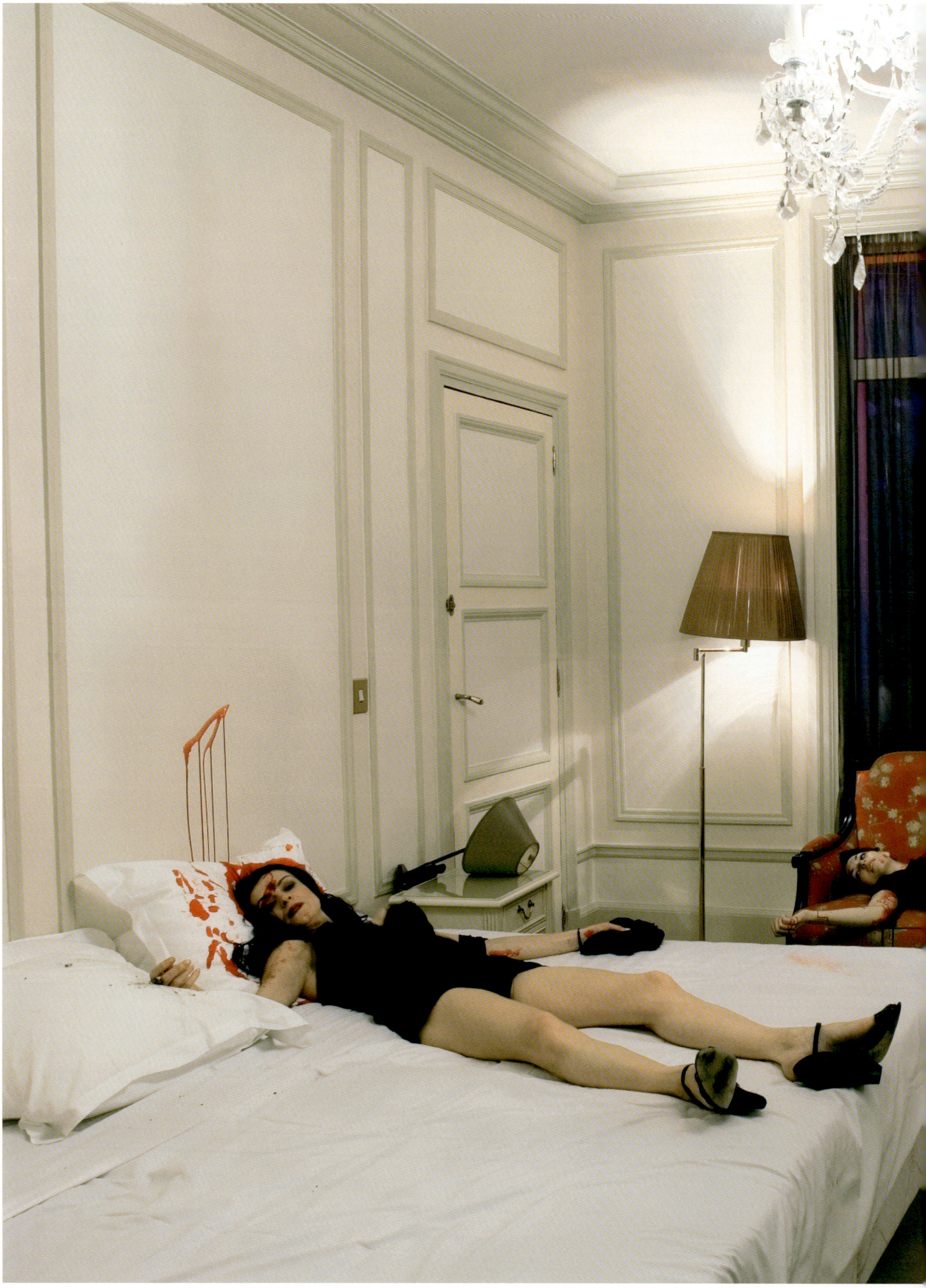

BLOODY MARY–VIRGINIE, DELPHINE, PÉNÉLOPE, 1993, with Philippe Perrin

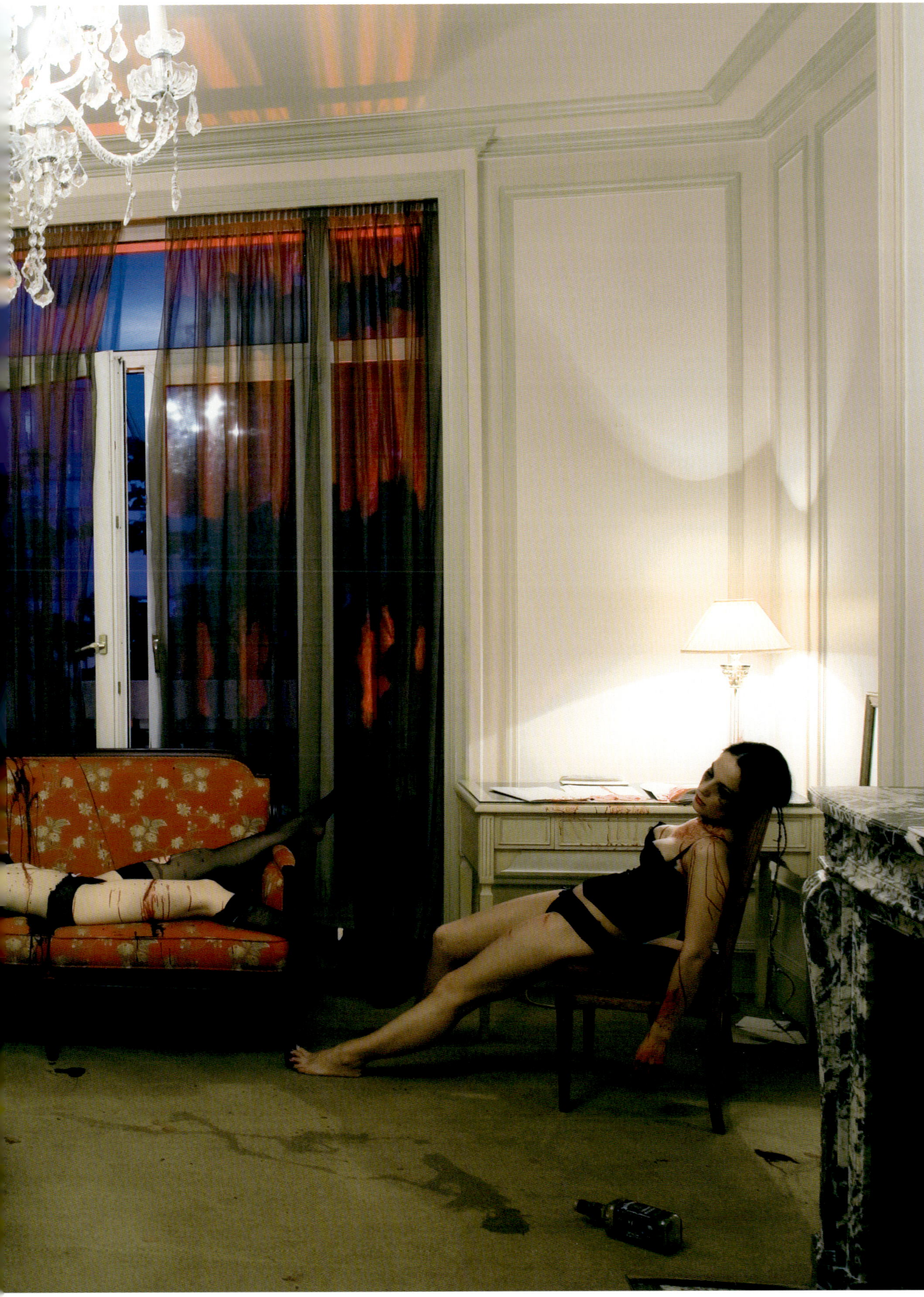

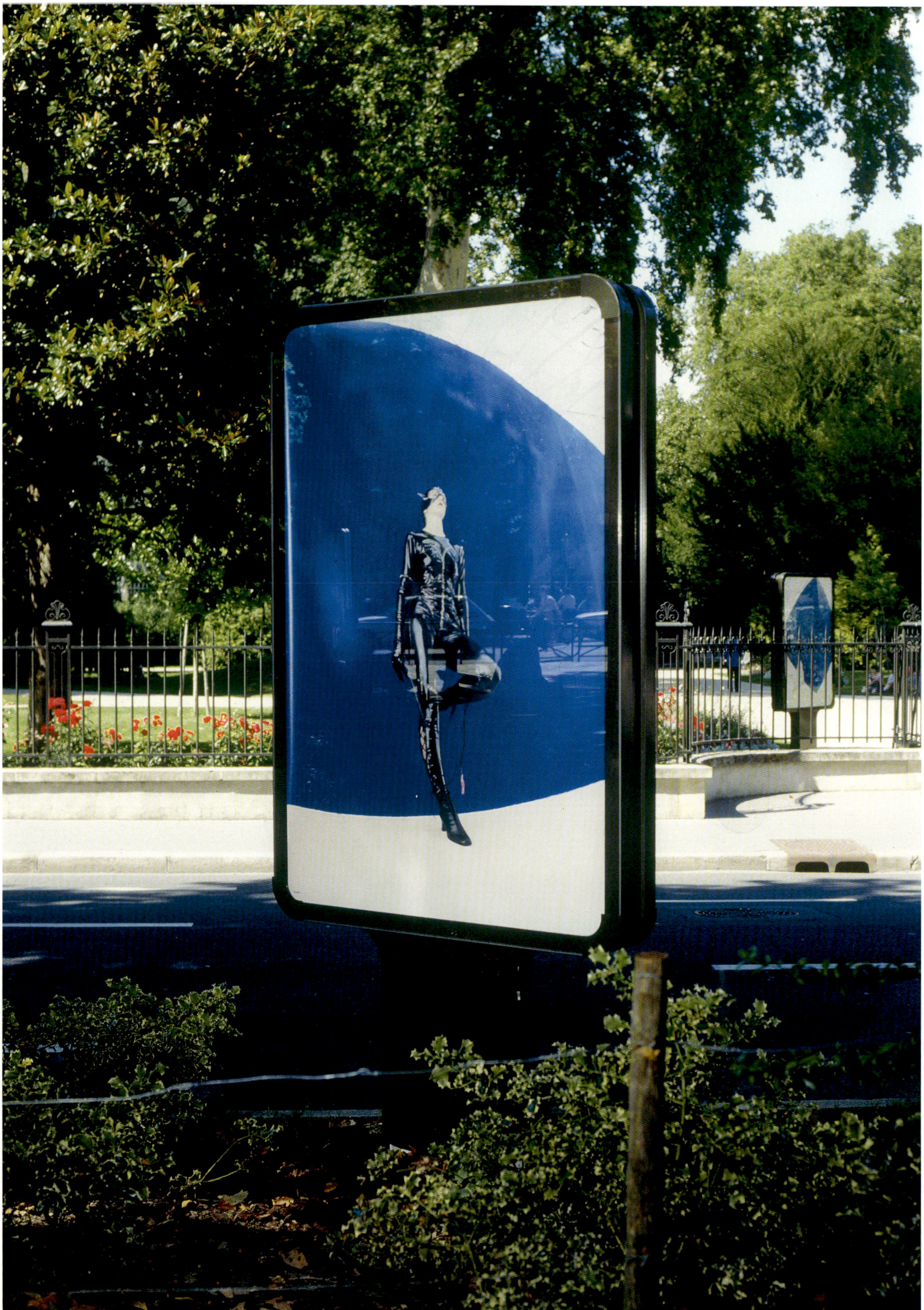

CATWOMAN, “Little Democracy” series, 1997

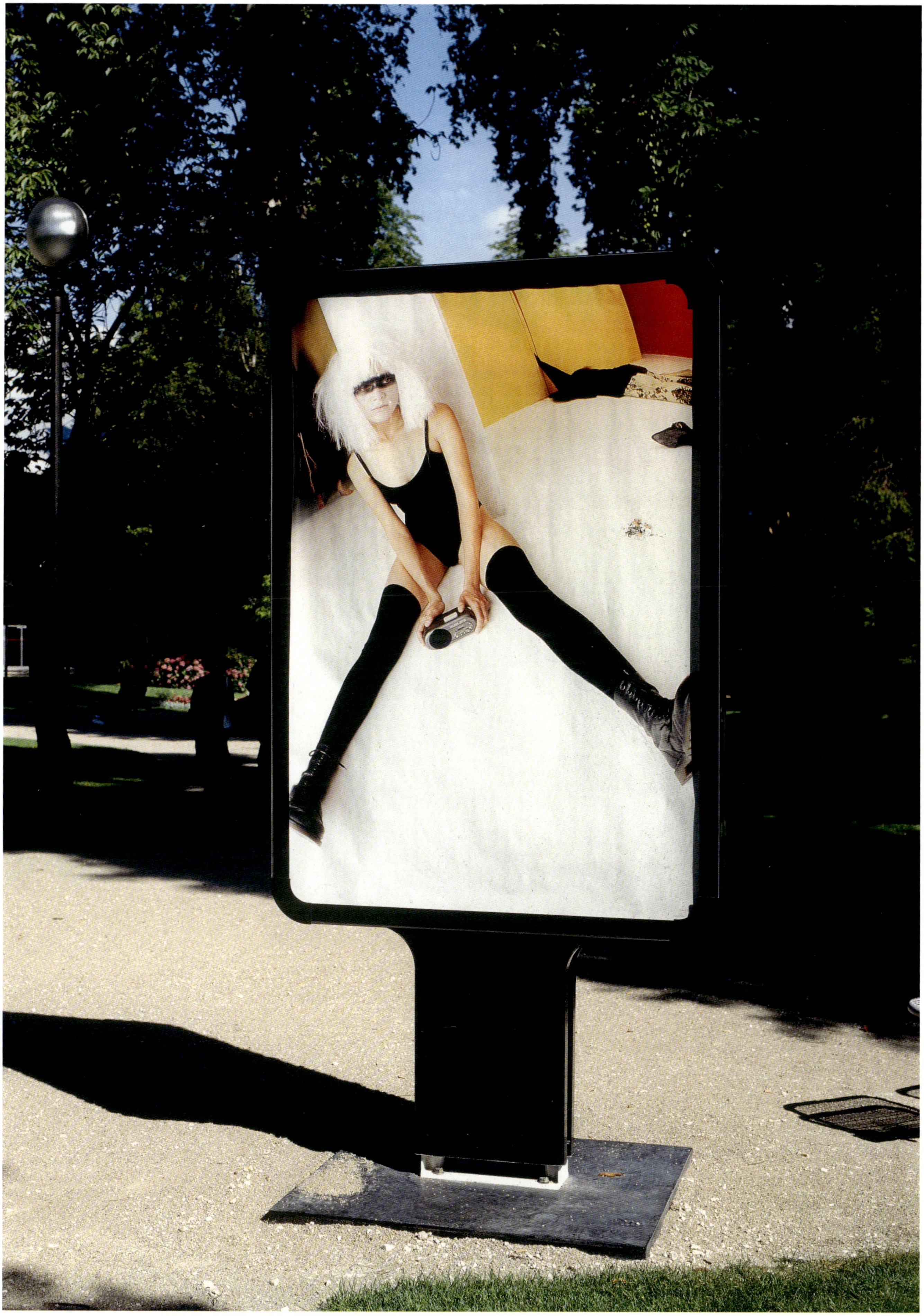

LA RÉPLIQUANTE, “Little Democracy” series, 1997

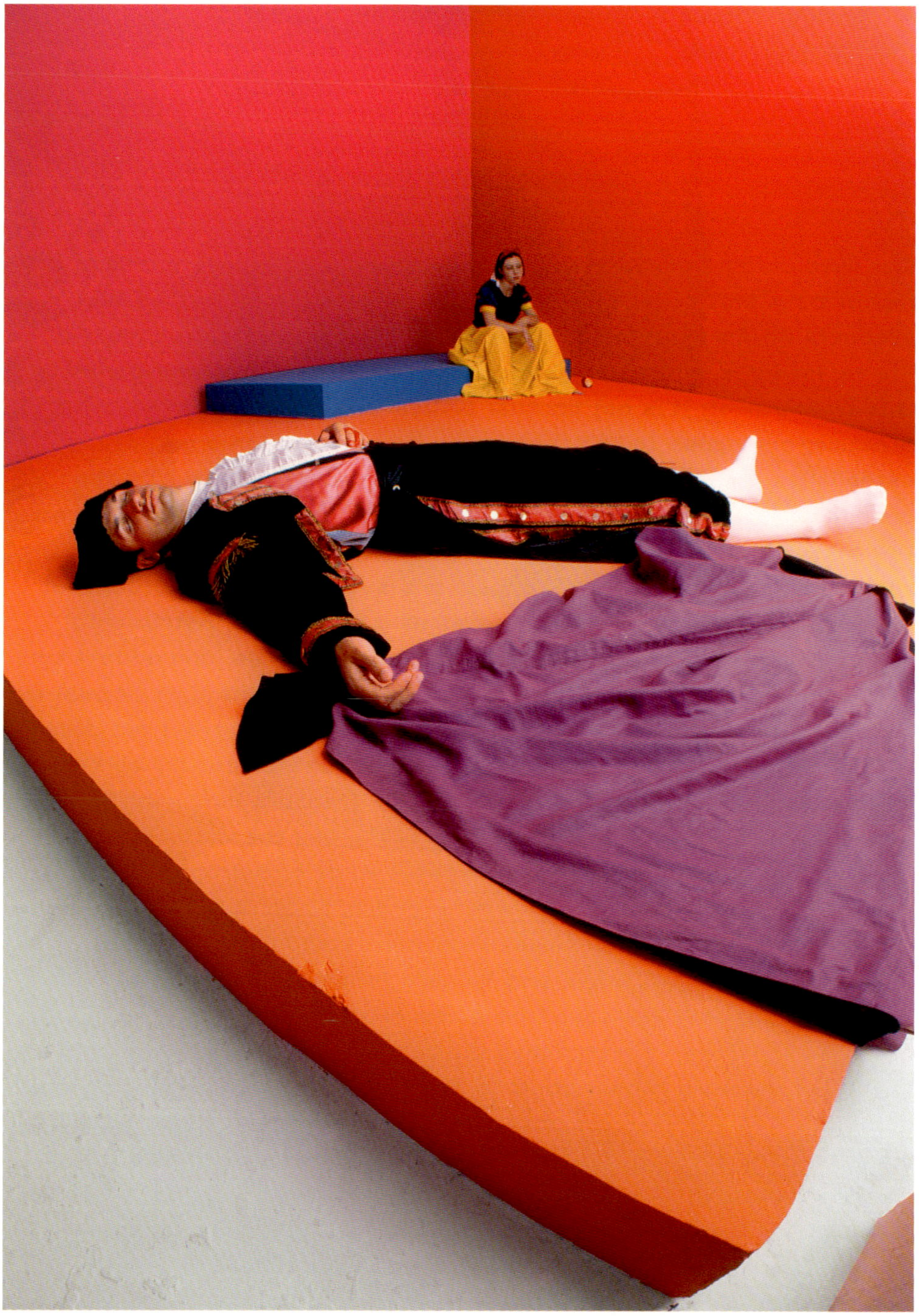

TORÉADOR, "Little Democracy" series, 1997

in an iconographic role play, wandering around the museum or the space of a group exhibition, surrounded by other works: after Duchamp, who intended to "use a Rembrandt as an ironing board," Joseph places his characters amid modern art that has become decor. His work always aims for the horizon of an exhibition in which the audience is hero: the art becomes a special effect in an interactive mise-en-scène. The process of reanimating the figure is twofold: it reanimates the works next to which the characters appear, and it makes the entire world a playground, a stage, or a set.

This system is also a political project: the artist speaks of the intelligent cohabitation of subjects and the backgrounds against which they move about, of the intelligent coexistence of human beings and the works

they are given to admire. The reanimation of icons, which characterizes the gallery of stock characters that make up "Little Democracy," represents a democratic form in its essence, without demagogy or ponderous demonstration. Joseph is suggesting that we inhabit pre-existing narratives and unceasingly refabricate the forms that suit us. Here the goal of the image is to introduce play-acting into systems of representation to keep them from becoming frozen, to detach forms from the alienating background where they become stuck if we take them for granted.
A superficial reading of the characters might lead one to believe that Joseph is an artist of the unreal, of popular entertainments. Yet the fairy-tale figures, cartoon characters, and science-fiction heroes that populate this democracy do not call for a flight from reality but urge us to experience our reality through fiction. In a complex stage management of live characters, Casper the Ghost, Cupid, and the fairy function as so many images *embedded* in the system of the division of labor: these imaginary beings, Joseph explains, obey "a cyclical, controlled, and unchanging program," and their functional status hardly differs from that of an assembly line worker at Renault, or a waiter in a restaurant who takes an order, serves a meal, and brings the bill. These characters are extremely typecast; they are robot-portraits, images perfectly associated with a model character, with a defined function. The true mythology from which they arise is the ideology of the division of labor and the standardization of products. The realm of the imaginary, indexed to the regime of production, indiscriminately affects plumbers and superheroes. The fairy illuminates things with her magic wand, the auto worker adjusts parts on an assembly line: work is the same everywhere, and it is this world of unchanging processes and potential dead ends that Joseph describes; images provide a way out.

The images Joseph offers must be experienced: they must be appropriated and reactivated, and included in new arrangements. In other words, meanings must be displaced. And tiny shifts create enormous movements. Why do so many artists strive to remake, recopy, dismantle, and reconstruct the components of our visual universe? What makes Pierre Huyghe reshoot Hitchcock and Pasolini? What compels Philippe Parreno to reconstruct an assembly line intended for leisure? To produce an alternative space and time, that is, to reintroduce the multiple and the possible into the closed circuit of the social, and for this, the artist must go back as far as possible in the collective machinery. With the help of installations that affect the exhibition site, Joseph offers us experimental objects, active products, and artworks that suggest new ways of apprehending the real and new types of investment in the art world. "Little Democracy" is something we can inhabit.

This text is excerpted from Nicolas Bourriaud, *Postproduction—Culture as Screenplay: How Art Reprograms the World*, Lukas & Sternberg, New York 2002, p. 62–66.

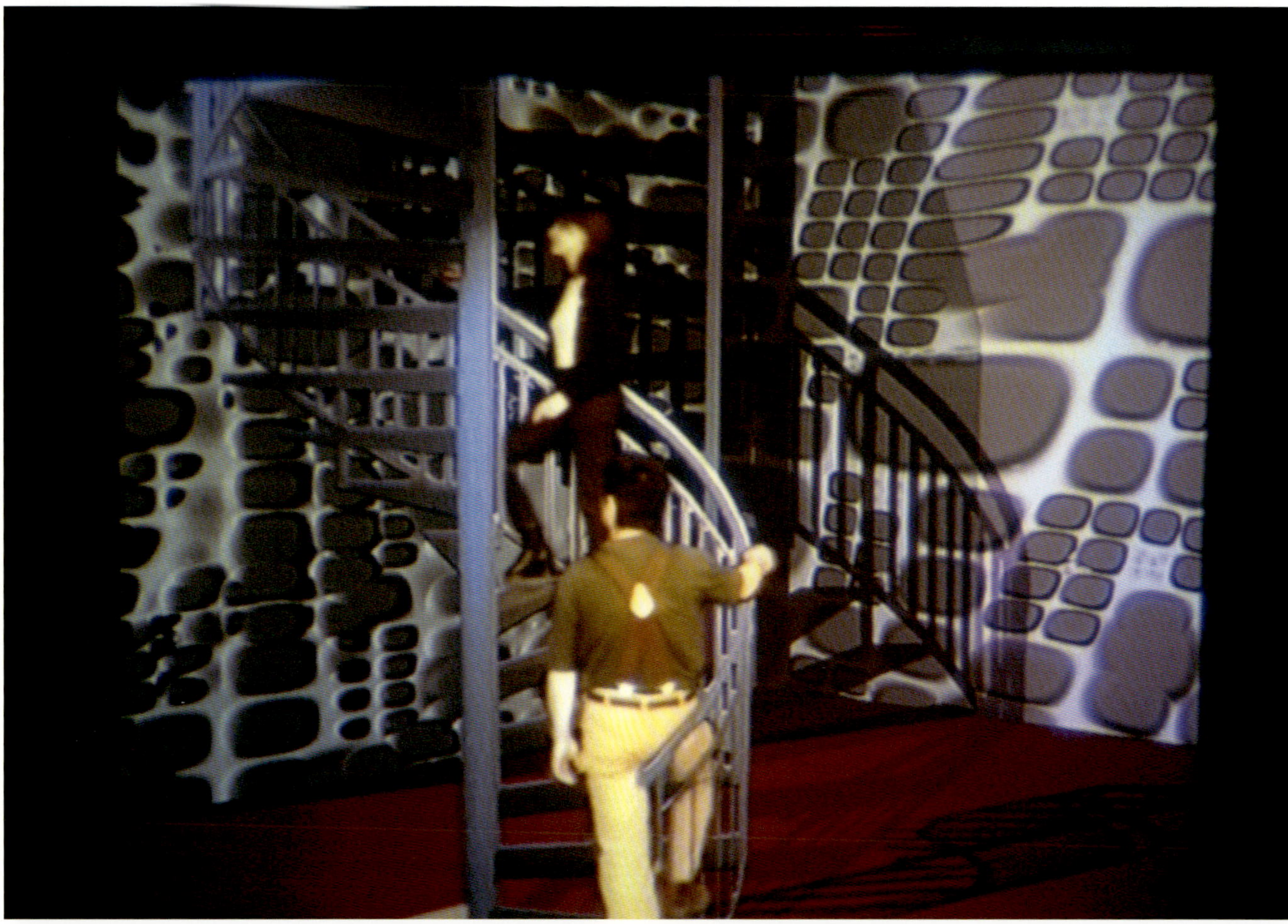

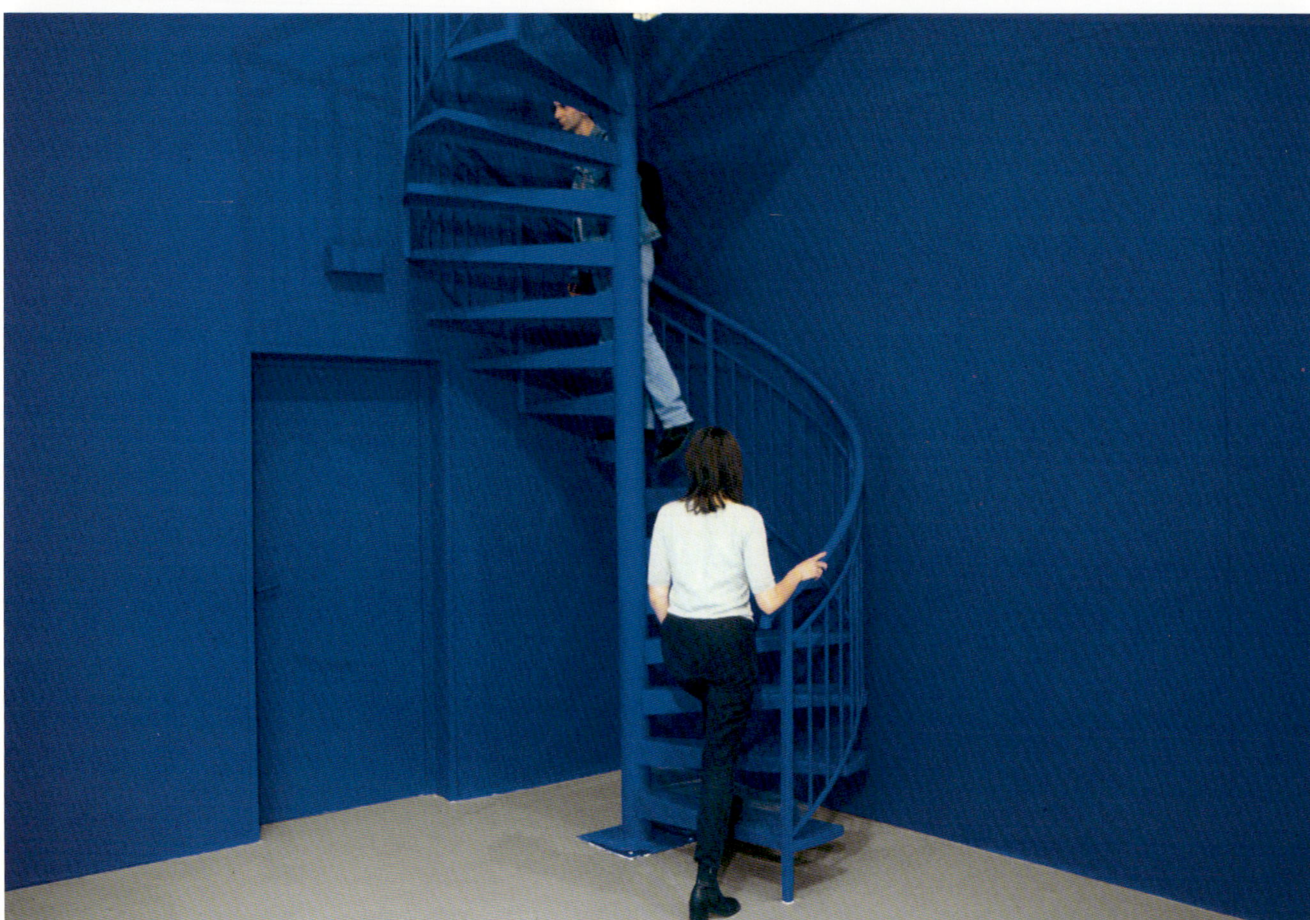

INCRUSTATION STONEWALL, 1997

A Percolation of Ideas and Activities
Pierre Joseph in Conversation with Liam Gillick

LIAM GILLICK When we first met in 1990 I was trying out some simple structural artwork in the space of Air de Paris in Nice, and with a wry smile you said: "Why would we want to see that? We know it already." I think there was an interesting ambiguous truth in this statement that is applicable to the failure of all contemporary art. And you always seemed to me to be very clear about rejecting certain orthodoxies in both subject and intention. There appears to be such a strong desire in your early work to address the present, but not in a formalistic way. Can you explain how you got to this point at such an early period?

PIERRE JOSEPH I think it's a question of education and context. My parents were photographers and my brother is a graphic designer, one of my uncles is a painter, and each of them has been a model of inspiration for me in different ways and at different times. During my childhood, questions relating to form, light, and color were important subjects—even issues—in discussions in my circle: being part of it is what allowed and enabled me to say "I know" or "I understand," so being able to jump certain steps. I wanted to change this paradigm and get away from such formalism.

The education I received—firstly in an experimental junior high school based on the Freinet model, then from a particularly inspired arts teacher in high school, and finally with my training at the Grenoble Art School—definitely killed any idea of academism or repetition of forms. I looked elsewhere for models—but I wasn't the only one—in the here and now, and I wanted to make use of elements—of processes—borrowed from the movies, science, technologies, and even fashion in my work. You could call it a magazine culture.

I always wondered why the media, as a form, could address different fields of activity, different discourses, different images, whereas artists could only develop one form, one discourse. *We* claimed the right to zapping, to sampling, and to trajectories.

LIAM GILLICK In England we were told there was no contemporary art in France. I think there was even an exhibition in France with the same title. My desire to come to Nice to see you was because I was not convinced about this absence of art, as I had already followed IFP and Ange Leccia, but I also felt strongly that maybe people could not see the art that was being made. It evaded all sentimental notions of poetics and various codes coming from the 1960s. Your work was the first I saw—alongside that of Philippe Parreno, Dominique Gonzalez-Foerster, and others—that seemed to really work in relation to recent contemporary theory. It was something completely new. What were you reading in the late 1980s—and if not reading, then absorbing (TV, cinema, design, etc.)? Were you aware of this newness?

PIERRE JOSEPH Yes and no. There was indeed an exhibition called *Il n'y pas d'art français* [There is No French Art], which took the shape of a journal—*Public*, edited by Philippe Cazal and Nadine Descendre—to which Bernard Joisten, Philippe Parreno, and I contributed. But this title has a different meaning to "there is no contemporary art in France." This publication was actually very close to reflections that came afterward about exhibition formats.
I offer you this list of elements that were absorbed in the late 1980s:

SIBERIA, 1988
with Bernard Joisten and Philippe Parreno

- Jean Baudrillard, Paul Virilio
- Gianni Vattimo, *Il pensiero debole* [The Weak Thought] (1983)
- *La Recherche*, *Sciences et Avenir* and other popular science magazines
- *Actuel*
- *ID*, *The Face*
- The Imagina annual shows in Monte-Carlo, which introduced reflections about virtual worlds
- The movie *Abyss* and movies by Lars von Trier—*Epidemic* (1987) and, earlier, *The Element of Crime* (1984)
- A certain book about special effects by Georges Lucas and Industrial Light & Magic, an American special effects company
- Video games
- Jeff Koons and Haim Steinbach in the La Caixa exhibition in Barcelona—or rather, its catalogue (1991)
- The Pompidou Centre catalogue *Les Immatériaux* (1985)
- The early exhibitions at the Cité des Sciences et de l'Industrie in Paris and those at La Casemate in Grenoble, especially because of their lay-outs and museography
- The Musée de l'Homme in Paris
- The big fairs and trade shows
- What Jean-Paul Gaultier, Marithé & François Girbaud, and, a little later, Martin Margiela were able to do in fashion
- House music and its various manifestations
- General Idea, Group Material, Collins & Milazzo and *The New Poverty* (New Observations, New York 1987).

With this search for external models came the idea of making and showing objects and situations that didn't look like art, which would have been a guarantee of novelty. The introduction of these external elements was what gave the impression of complete novelty. That might be one of the differences from the avant-garde that managed to produce works out of nothing; my—our—work had more to do with import-export, the transposition or the translation of preexisting elements.

LIAM GILLICK You have used maps or guides that are out of sync with what is being mapped. Creating new cartographies but not psycho-geographies in the Situationist sense. Am I wrong?

PIERRE JOSEPH It's more literal in fact; it's the result of making a drawing from memory. It's a question of adapting, or not, to a challenging reality, and an indirect way of letting some individual subjectivity come through, when it's not complete irrationality. I was simply wondering about individual knowledge, how you transform, how you forget, and what you remember.

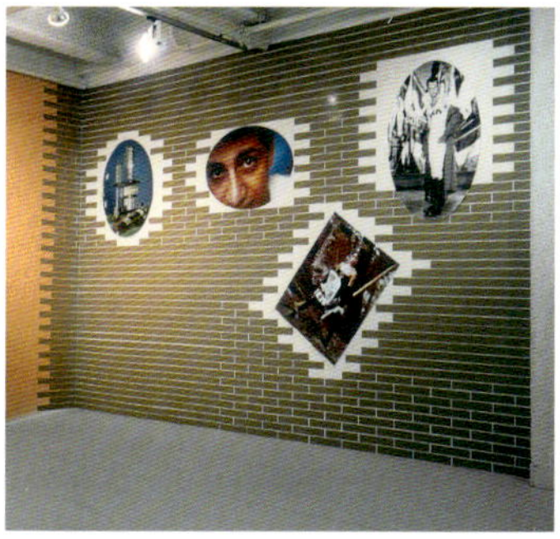

COMPOSIT, 1988
with Bernard Joisten and Philippe Parreno

In England, I think the artist Emma Kay has done similar work, going so far as to transcribe the Bible from memory—and of course, there is no need to mention Robert Morris' work; I saw that in the catalogue for the *Abracadabra* show at Tate Britain in London (1999). Another catalogue ...

LIAM GILLICK The play with characters that recurs in your work appears to anticipate other artists' obsessions with subjectivities—but yours always appear completely synthetic.

PIERRE JOSEPH It's the notion of reactivation that kept me going: doing something again. The notion of reactivation—and the word—emerged when I took the photograph of the first character I produced: is it a trace, or is it the beginning of something? I thought of it as a video game; you must be able to play the game again as you please. The word "reactivation" comes from that, nobody was using it at the time in contemporary art. To reproduce a character, of which I made an image, from that image, is what I call a reactivation. But it can also be understood in a broad sense: the Beast (from *The Beauty and the Beast* by Jean Cocteau) or Snow White don't belong to me. I reactivate in that sense as well; I reactivate a collective memory of other authors' work.

LIAM GILLICK There appears to be a commitment to playing with forms of pedagogy in your work that removes it from the direct context of participatory work that has emerged in the last few years. Can you explain your role in relation to younger artists?

PIERRE JOSEPH I have organized lots of workshops with art-school students, who have been able to give me material for various exhibitions. So sometimes I use their work when the initial hypothesis is imagined by me and I have a plan on which it is based. I have worked with them on drawing from memory in order to test the universality of representations and of knowledge experienced at the individual level: the world map, the human digestive system, or more intimately, representations of sexual parts, male and female. What remains of it all after being filtered through thought and memory?

Another form of instrumentalization was one that I organized for my retrospective at the 2007 Lyon Biennial: I asked young artists to replay some of my works, with their own adaptation, based on the hypothesis that the result would be a continuation of my work. What I wanted to make felt in this play of transmission and authorship is the interchangeability of our productions and of our position as artists over time within the institutions.

Moreover, I also believe that students and artists—I am thinking of Bruno Persat, Christophe Sarlin—are able to formulate or to answer questions I'm asking myself and to push them further.

LIAM GILLICK Early collaboration in your work is replaced by you often working alone—this is true of many artists of our generation. What is your critique of collaborative strategies?

PIERRE JOSEPH It is a good way to become visible on the art scene; working as a group produces a real synergy and gives a certain weight to *peut-être* (*Yes, No, Maybe*, Les presses du réel, 2011). A work of art isn't necessarily a work of art only because the artist decides it is. It also belongs, or not, to an ensemble of art definitions, in a time of art schools and institutions, with a rotation of artists in these different structures.

LIAM GILLICK What is your reaction to the current interest in what is known in English as Speculative Realism in philosophy? Namely, the critique of the idea that we only have access to the correlation between thinking and being, and never to one apart from the other. At the root is a criticism of anthropocentrism—loosely the placing of the human at the center of things. It seems that some of these recent theories are required to understand your relationship to objects, scientific structures, and mapping in your work over the last twenty years.

PIERRE JOSEPH It's a little like asking yourself: does my work exist if nobody is there to look at it or buy it?

I think that it's not so much the work I'm making that I find interesting, but rather it's what it could describe in the long run. Regarding the characters, the idea of reactivation was stronger than the theatrical form that the presence of these extras could bring into an exhibition. What I retain from the works from memory, which anyone can make, is that I can try to link them to other elements I have produced: a table, a mirror, a manifesto. That texts about transmission could coexist with a witch squashed on a wall ... And this can echo this type of sentence: "The realm of things includes equal parts of objects that are physical (a quark) and theoretical (concepts), natural (a dog) and artificial (a computer), intangible (a multinational company), and concrete, real, and imaginary." As well as, "things become contingent: they may not exist." I feel like talking of contingency (there, not there) in relation to my work, or of meteorology. So, on this basis, yes, it gets interesting. There is no (more) sense, but rather a form of percolation of activities and information.

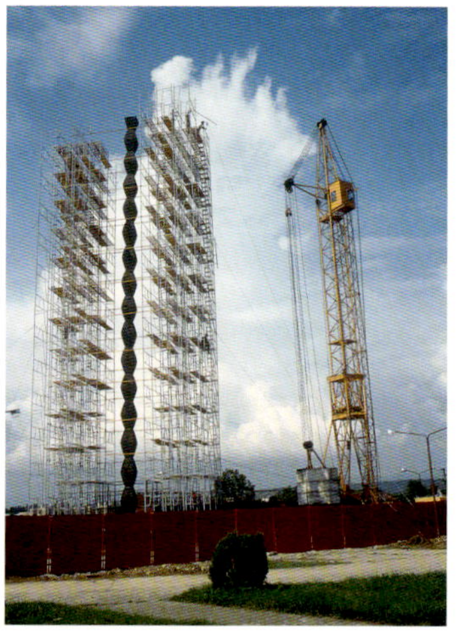

BRANCUSI RESTAURÉ I, 1996

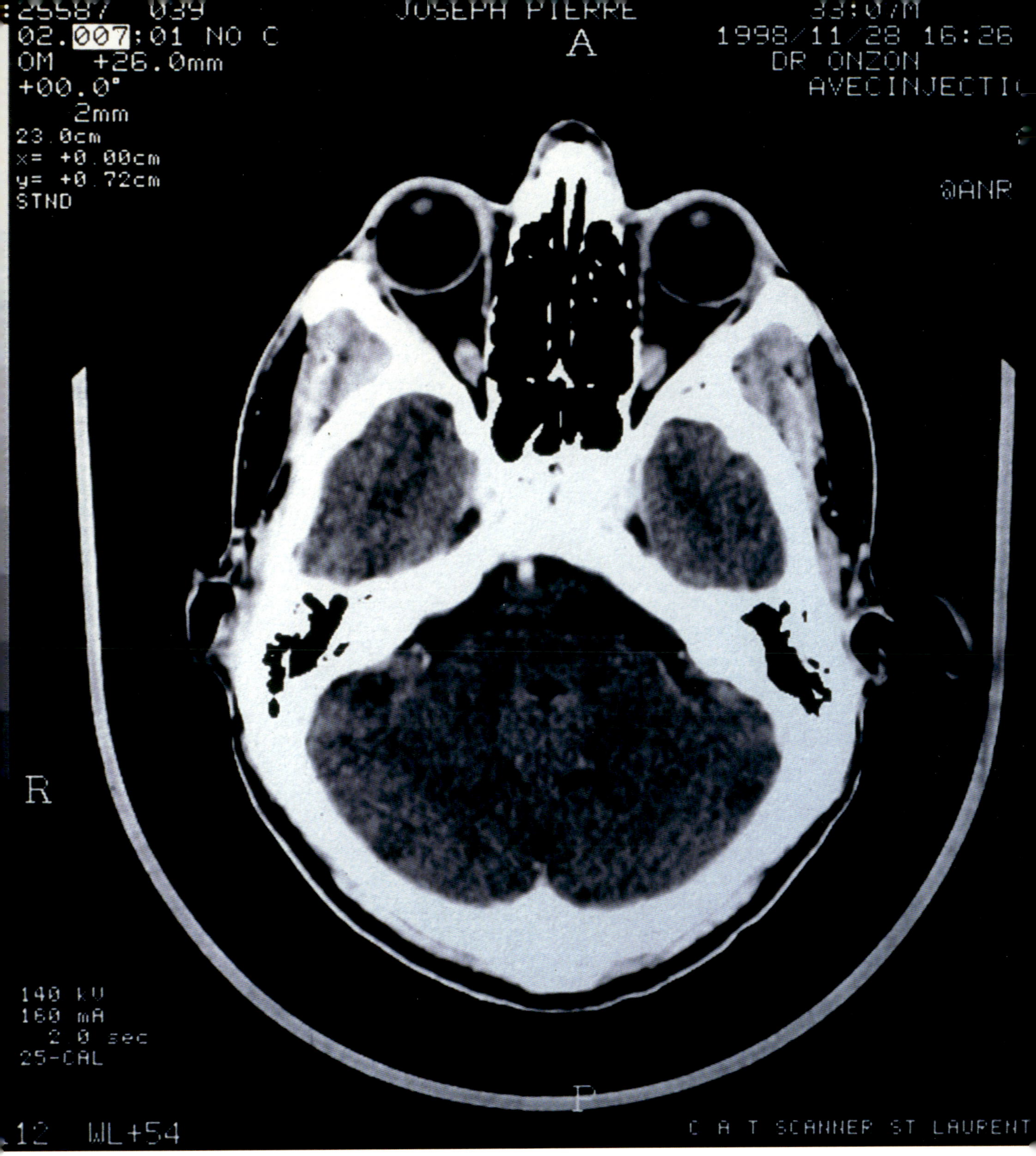

VOIR L'IMAGE DU CÔTÉ PRACTICIEN/MON CERVEAU, 1998

LEARNING BY EXPERIENCE, 1998

→

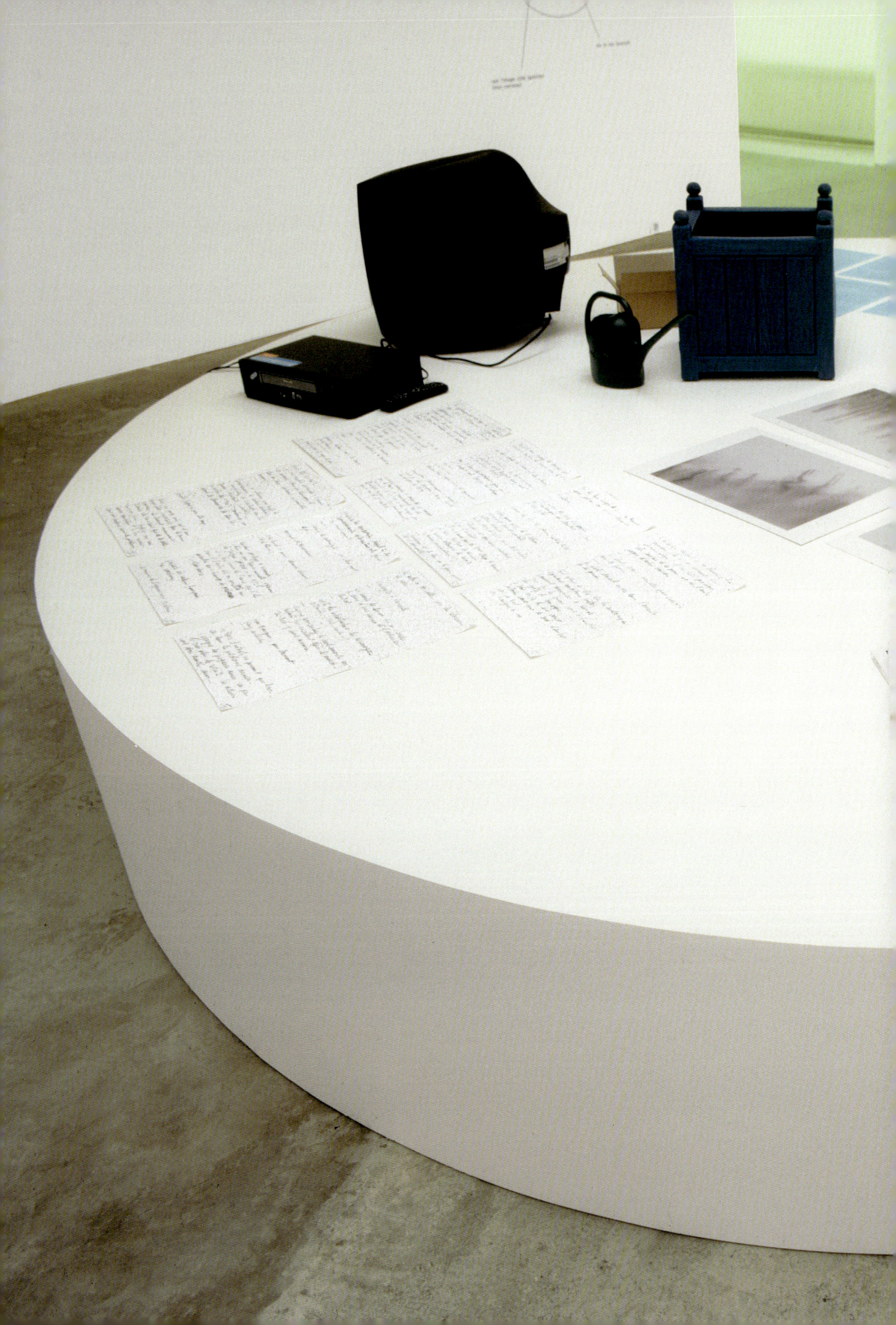

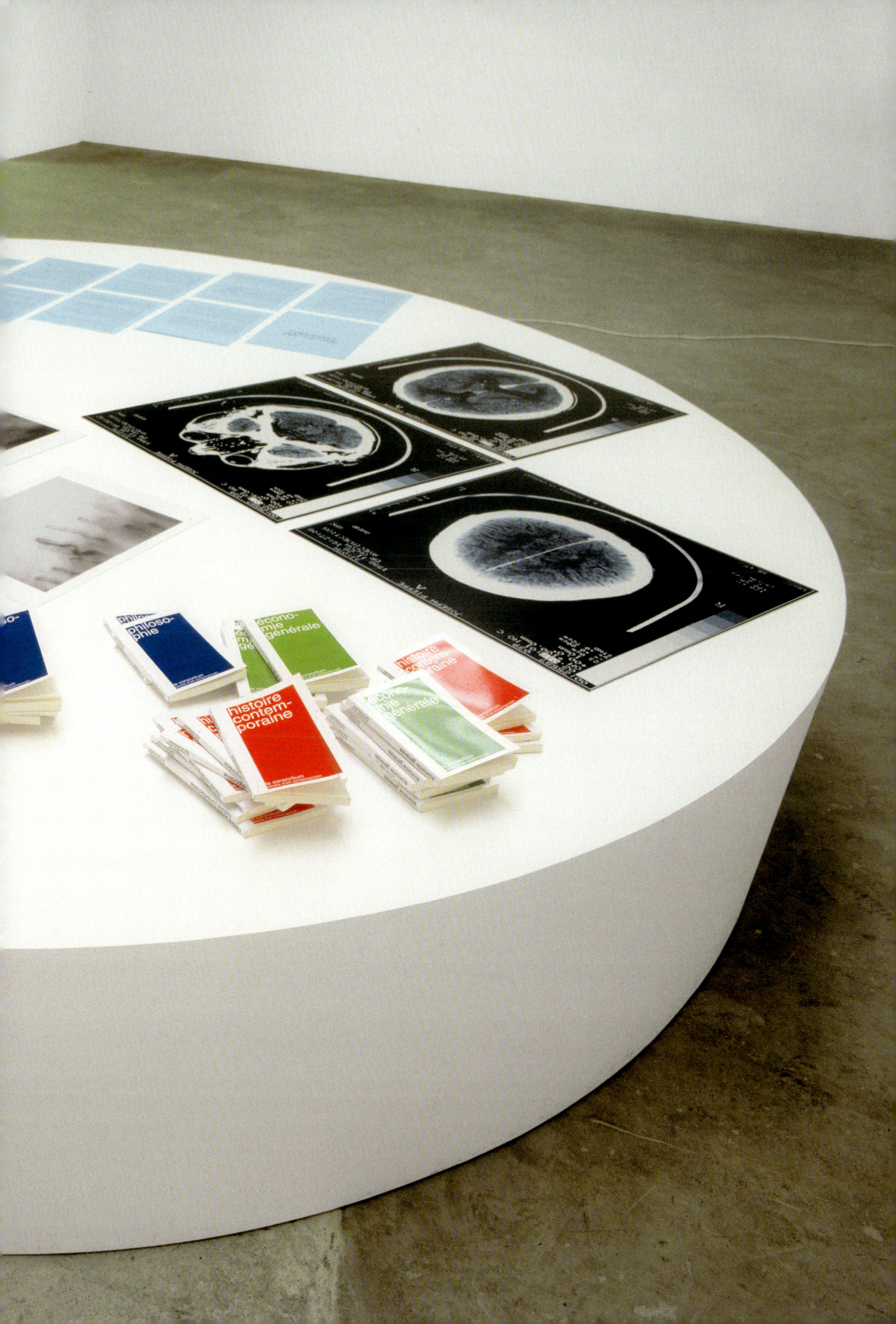

philoso-
phie
économie
générale
histoire
contem-
poraine
le consortium

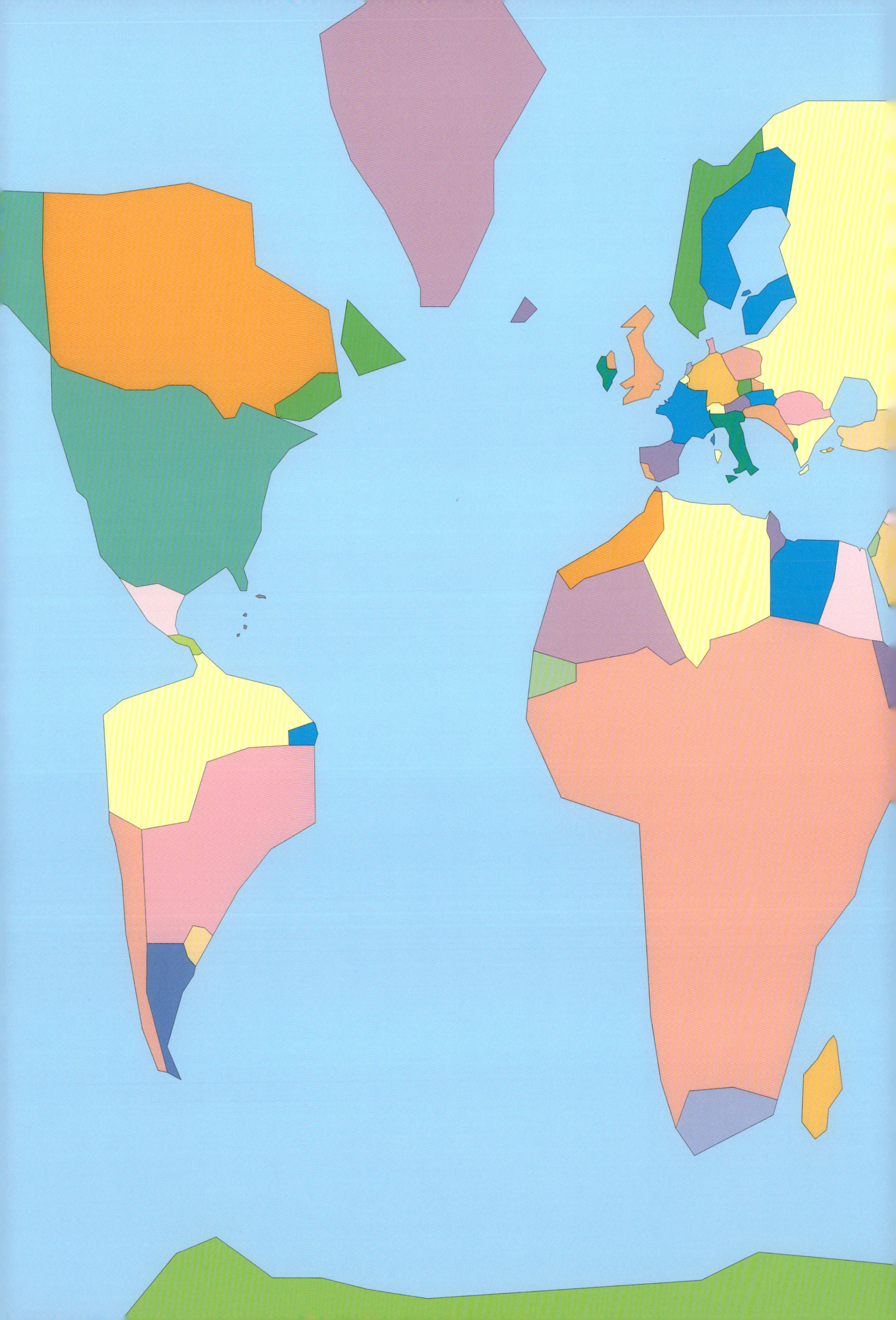

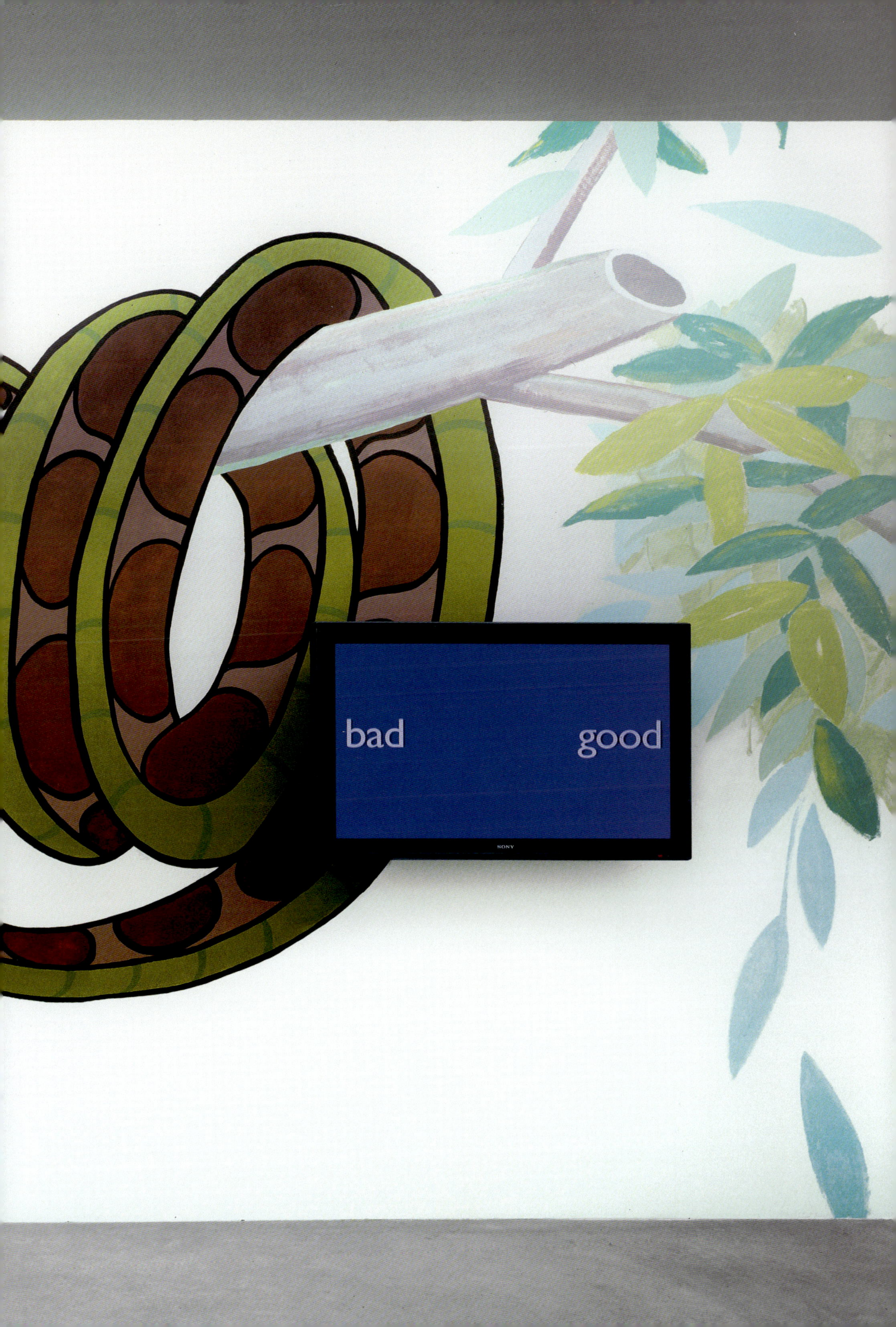
bad
good
SONY

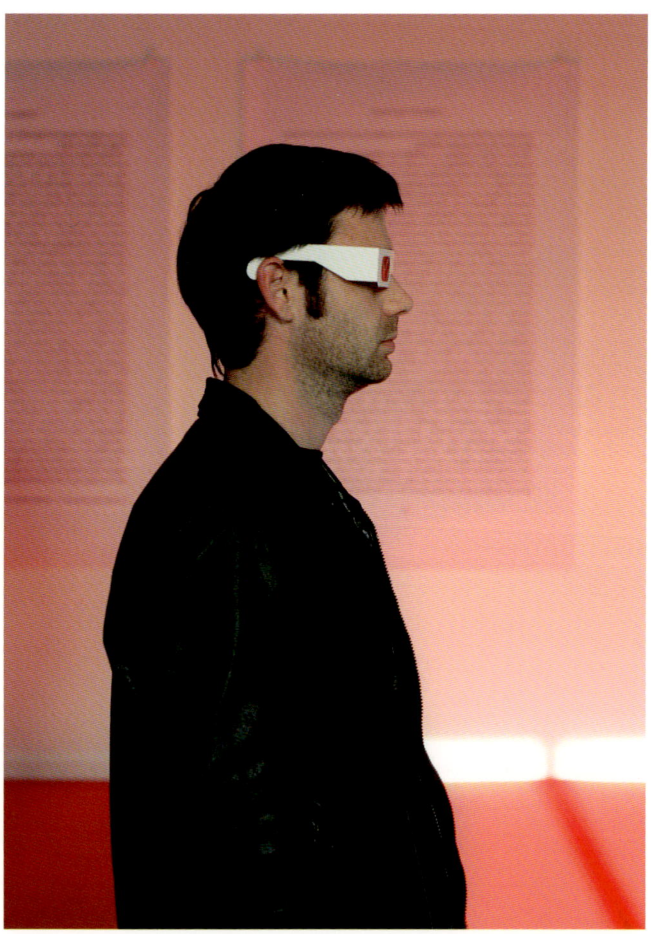

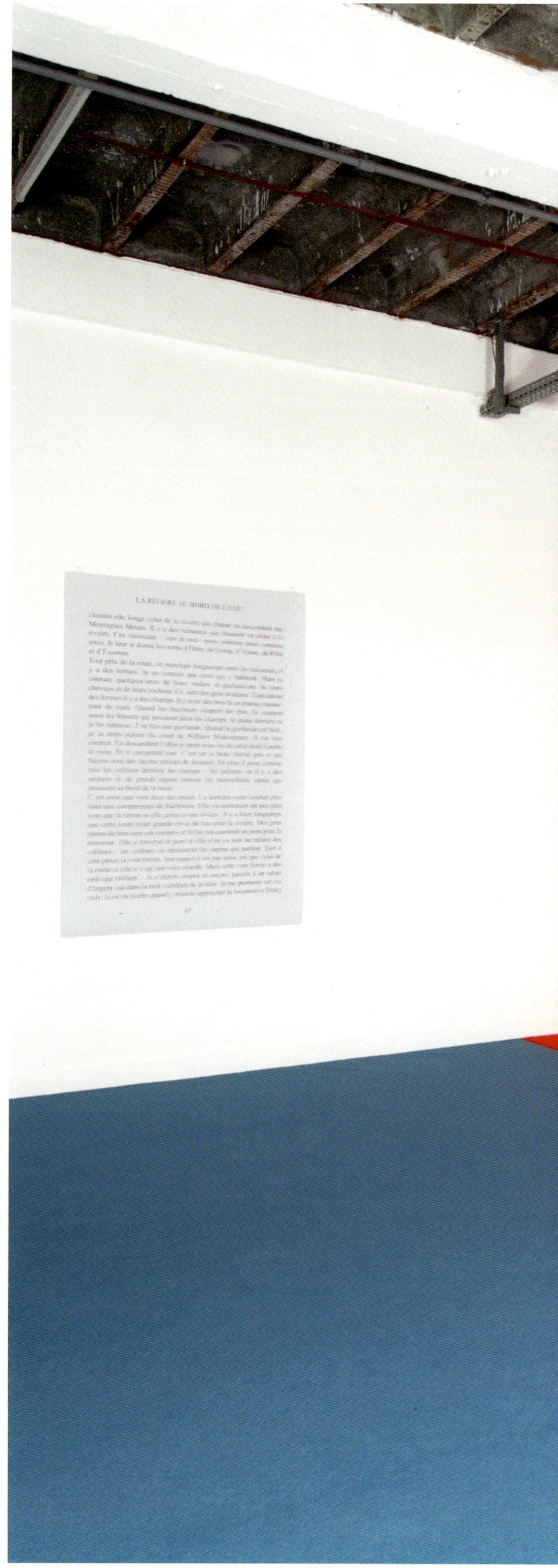

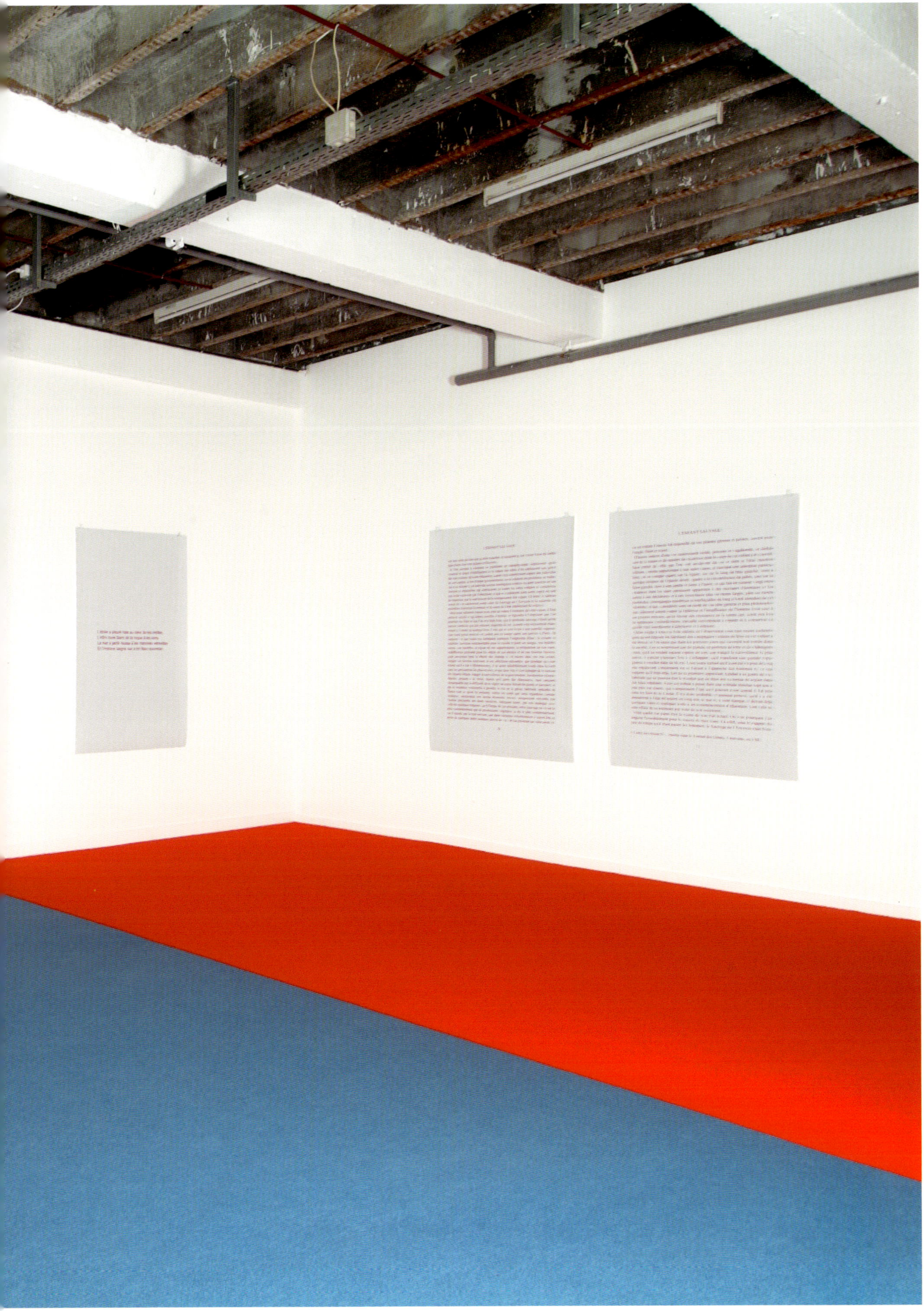

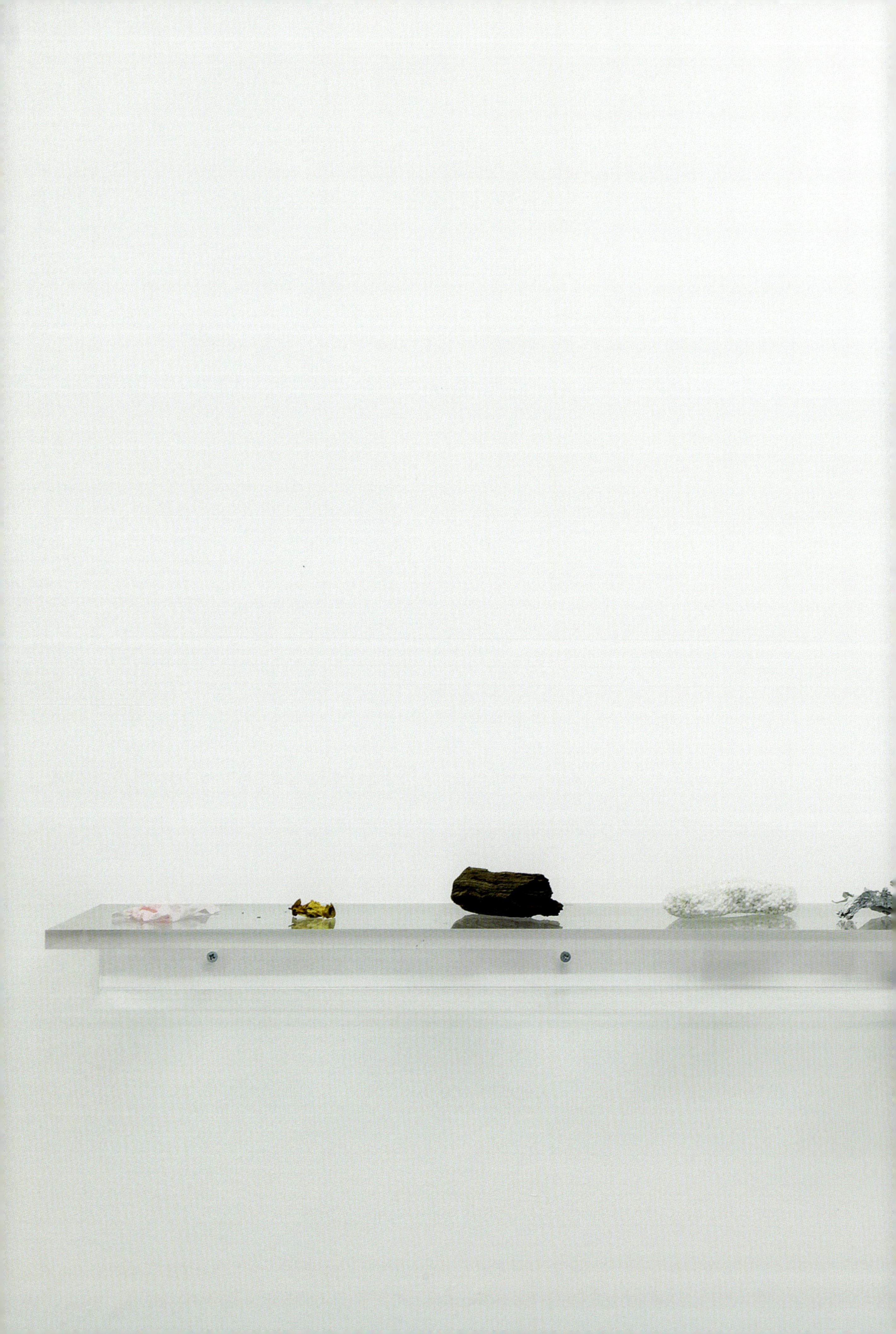

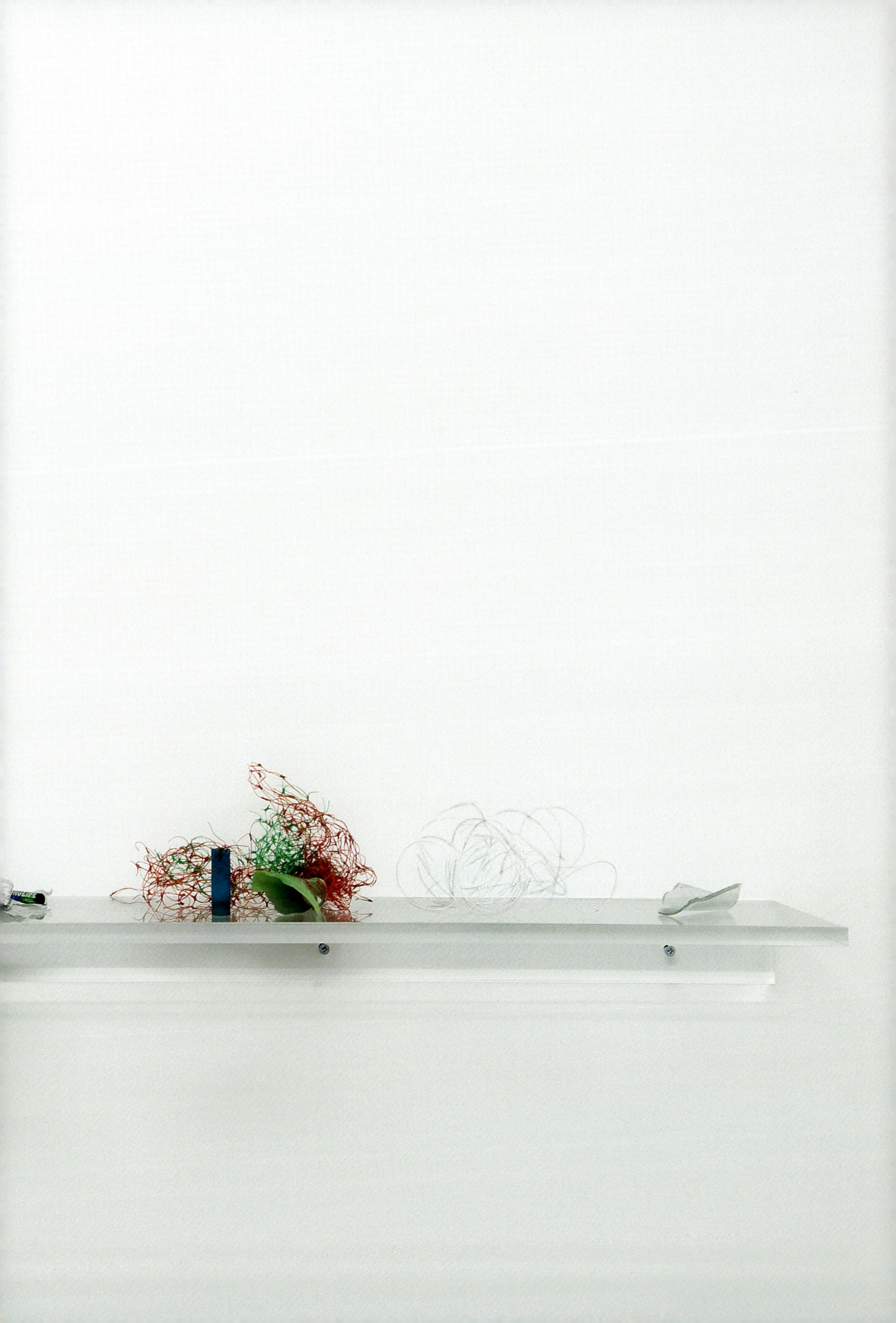

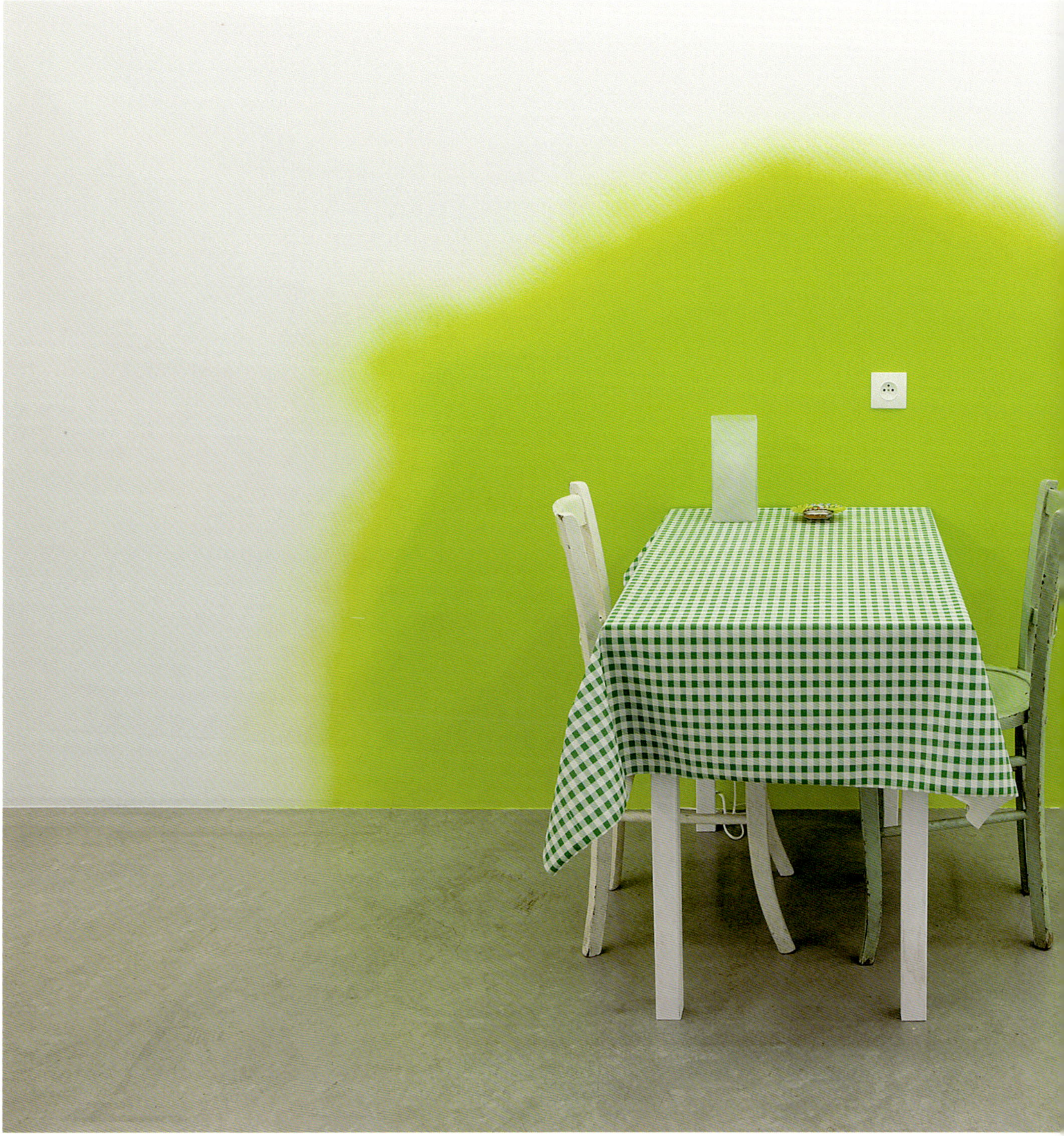

FROM APPLE CORE TO GLASS, 2010
←

LÀ, PAS LÀ (TABLE), 2010

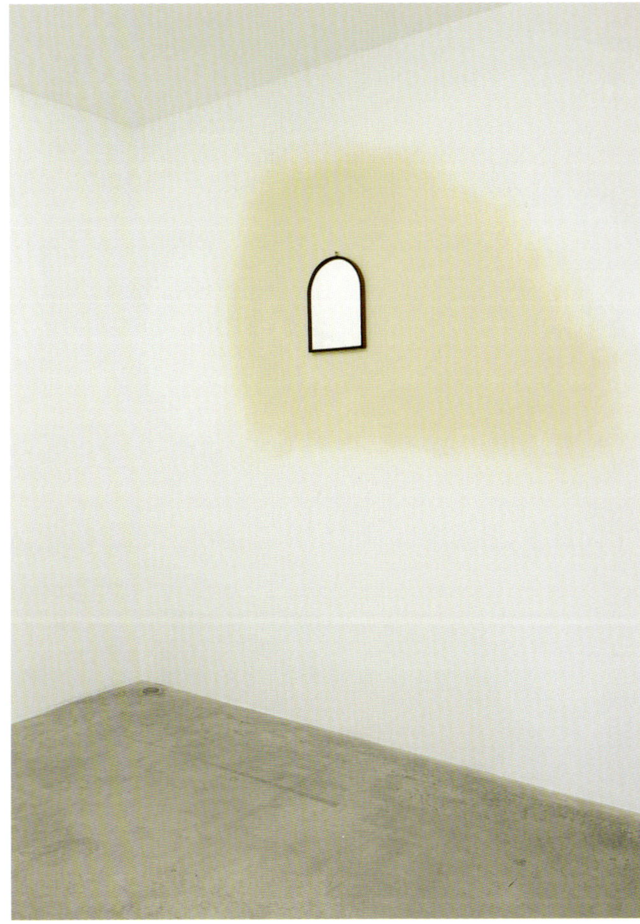

LÀ, PAS LÀ (MIROIR), 2010

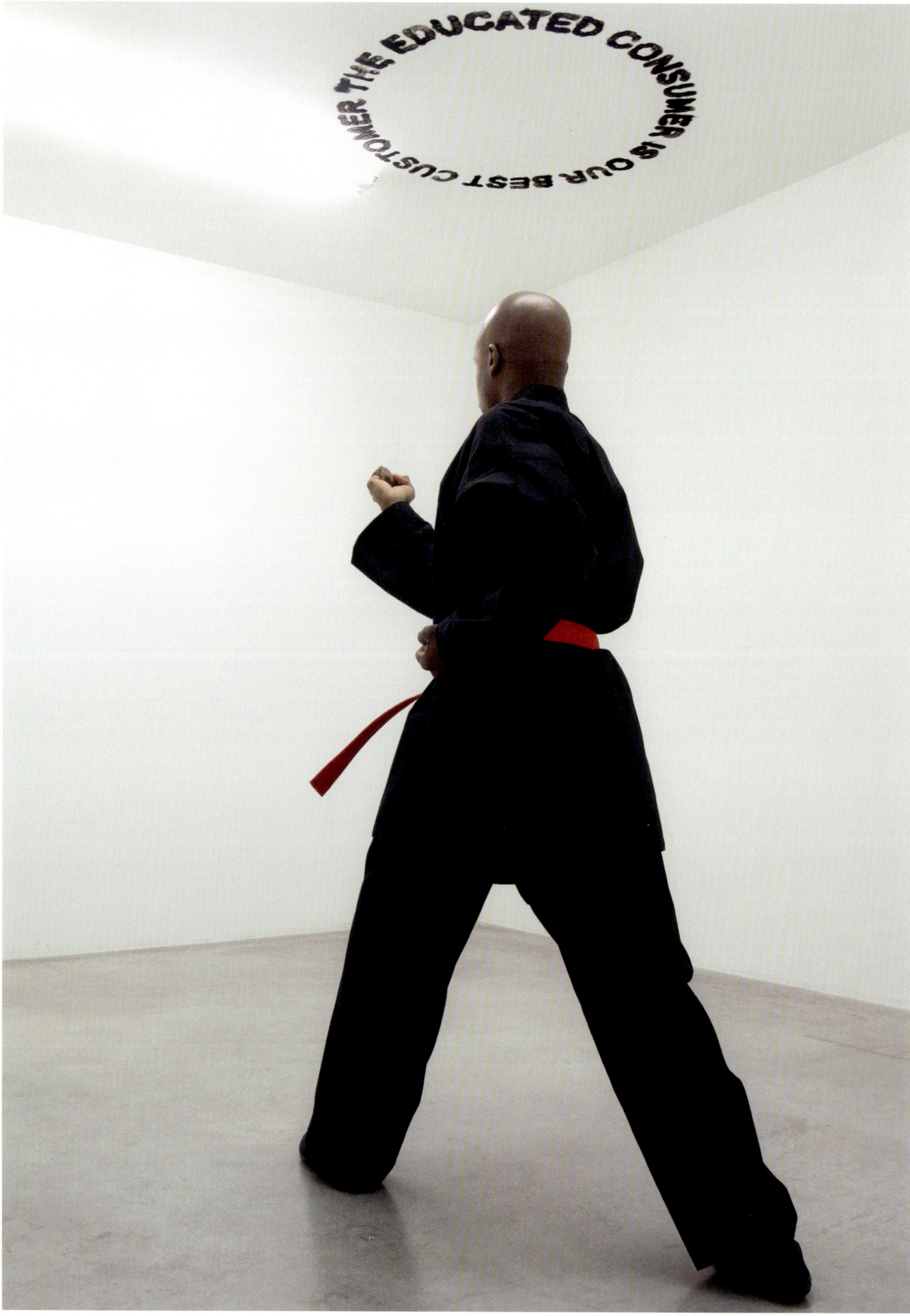

MANGA (PERSONNAGE À RÉACTIVER), 1997–2007

Biography

1965
Born in Caen, Pierre Joseph lives and works in Paris.

A retrospective monograph *Oui, non, peut-être* was published in 2011 by Les presses du réel (448 pages). It contains a catalogue raisonné of Pierre Joseph's works, as well as a critical anthology, and a complete bibliography.

SELECTED SOLO EXHIBITIONS

2010
From Apple Core to Glass, Air de Paris, Paris
2007
Pierre Joseph, Forde, Geneva
2006
Si ce monde vous déplaît, FRAC Poitou-Charentes, Angoulême
La Théorie du trickster, screening, Tate Modern, London
2003
Action restreinte, Palais de Tokyo, Paris
2002
La Théorie du trickster, with Mehdi Behlaj Kacem, Le Spot, Le Havre
1998
Pierre Joseph, Le Consortium, Dijon
1997
Little Democracy, Centre de création contemporaine (CCC), Tours
1995
Personnages à réactiver, FRAC Champagne-Ardennes, Reims/Le Parvis, Tarbes*
1993
La chasse au trésor ou l'aventure du spectateur disponible, Air de Paris, Paris
1991
Try Snaking, with Philippe Parreno, Air de Paris, Nice
1990
Ozone, with Bernard Joisten, Dominique Gonzalez-Foerster, and Philippe Parreno, FRAC Corse*
Les Ateliers du paradise, with Philippe Perrin and Philippe Parreno, Air de Paris, Nice
Once upon a Time in City Bild, with Philippe Parreno, Esther Shipper, Cologne
1989
Ozone, with Bernard Joisten, Dominique Gonzalez-Foerster, and Philippe Parreno, APAC, Nevers
Galerie intelligente, with Philippe Parreno, Galerie des Archives, Paris

SELECTED GROUP EXHIBITIONS

2012
Dallas Biennial, Dallas Contemporary, Dallas
2011
Collector: Œuvres du Centre national des Arts plastiques, Tripostal, Lille*
2010
Tricksters Tricked, Van Abbemuseum, Eindhoven
2009
Utopics: 11th Swiss Sculpture Exhibition, Biel*
Là où je suis n'existe pas, Printemps de Septembre, Toulouse*
2007
Destroy Athens: 1st *Athens Biennial*, Athens*
00s – L'Histoire d'une décennie qui n'est pas encore nommée: Contemporary Art Biennial, Institut d'art contemporain, Villeurbanne, Lyon*
2006
L'École de Stéphanie: La Force de l'art, Grand Palais, Paris*
Cinéma(s), Le Magasin, Grenoble*
2003
GNS (Global Navigation System), Palais de Tokyo, Paris*
2002
No Ghost Just a Shell, Van Abbemuseum, Eindhoven/ SFMOMA, San Francisco/Kunsthalle, Zürich*
2000
Au-delà du spectacle, Centre Pompidou, Paris*
Présumés innocents: L'art contemporain et l'enfance, CAPC, musée d'art contemporain, Bordeaux*
1992
Il faut construire l'hacienda, Centre de création contemporaine (CCC), Tours*

* Publication

List of Works Reproduced

Cover
Le Toréador (Personnage à réactiver), 1994
Reactivation view in the exhibition *Le sort probable de l'homme qui avait avalé le fantôme*, La Conciergerie, Centre Pompidou Nouveau Festival, 2009
Marc & Josée Gensollen Collection, Marseille

Endleaves
Atlas, images restaurées. Sexe féminin-Vue anatomique, 2005
Atlas, images restaurées. Sexe masculin-Vue anatomique, 2005
FRAC Languedoc-Roussillon Collection, Montpellier

[p. 1] *Cache-cache*, 1990
Exhibition view, *A Christmas Show*, Air de Paris, Nice, 1990
Fabric, katana sword, smart card, Reebok trainers, 100 × 100 × 20 cm
20 versions with different colors, weapons, and shoe sizes

[p. 2] *Les Voleurs de couleurs (Personnages à réactiver)*, 1992
Created for the exhibition *That's all ... my friends*, Galerie Montaigne, Paris, 1992
Cibachrome mounted on aluminum, 90 × 120 cm
Loïc Malle Collection, Monaco; Private Collection, Monaco

[p. 5] *Si ce monde vous déplaît*, 2006
Exhibition views, FRAC Poitou-Charentes, Angoulême, 2006
15th-century *Pieta* (Anonymous, Musée d'Angers), aluminum cans, three videos on flat screens, stickers, variable dimensions
FRAC Poitou-Charentes Collection, Angoulême

[p. 7] *Table sans nom*, 2004
Painted resin top and metallic base, 140 × 243 × 81 cm
Fonds municipal d'art contemporain Collection, Paris
With Stéphanie Moisdon
Scenery for *L'École de Stéphanie*, Artissima, Lingotto, Turin, 2008
Scenery for *L'École de Stéphanie*, *La Force de l'Art*, Grand Palais, Paris, 2006

[p. 9] *Rétrospective*, 2007
Exhibition view, *00s. L'Histoire d'une décennie qui n'est pas encore nommée*, Lyon Contemporary Art Biennial, musée d'Art contemporain, Lyon, 2007
Digital label on flat screen
Exhibition view, *00s. L'Histoire d'une décennie qui n'est pas encore nommée*, Lyon Contemporary Art Biennial, musée d'Art contemporain, Lyon, 2007
Installation view of Raphaël Zarka's *Riding Modern Art* participation, a photographic collection about Katarzyna Kobro's *Spatial Composition 3* (1928), photographs by Éric Antoine, Loïc Benoît, Sébastien Charlot, Guillaume Langlois, Dominic Marley, Bertrand Trichet, Marcel Veldman, and Alexis Zavialoff
[For Raphaël Zarka's works:
Courtesy Galerie Michel Rein, Paris]

[p. 10–11] *Mallette Hyper Hyper*, 1988
With Dominique Gonzalez-Foerster, Bernard Joisten, and Philippe Parreno
Mecanorma plastic briefcase with "Hyper Hyper" sticker, 42 × 43 × 9 cm
Five plastified color Xeroxes, 29.2 × 40.8 cm each
Collections: Nicolas Bourriaud, Paris; Emmanuel Perrotin, Paris; Esther Schipper, Berlin
Bottom left: *Hyper Hyper*, 1988
Color Xerox, 42 × 60 cm
Hervé Acker Collection, Paris

[p. 12] *Video Ozone*, 1989
With Dominique Gonzalez-Foerster, Bernard Joisten, and Philippe Parreno
Exhibition view, *De l'instabilité*, Centre national des arts plastiques, Paris, 1989
Video installation, giant TV-screen-like inflatable structure, 500 × 700 × 400 cm; duration: 4'55
Filmmaker: François Reymond
Music: S'Express, *Coma II*, with the kind authorization of Rhythm King
Fonds national d'art contemporain Collection, Puteaux

[p. 13] *Ozone*, 1989
Exhibition view, *Ozone*, APAC, Nevers, 1989
With Dominique Gonzalez-Foerster, Bernard Joisten, and Philippe Parreno
Giant slides, 100 × 100 cm each
FRAC Corse Collection, Corte
Sac Ozone, 1988
With Dominique Gonzalez-Foerster, Bernard Joisten, and Philippe Parreno
Backpack with various elements (balloons, documentation, aerosol, etc.)
FRAC Corse Collection, Corte

[p. 14–15] *Les Ateliers du Paradise*, 1990
With Philippe Parreno and Philippe Perrin
Exhibition views, *Les Ateliers du Paradise. A film in real time by Pierre Joseph, Philippe Parreno, and Philippe Perrin*, Air de Paris, Nice, 1990
Invitation card, 1990
Trampoline, 1990
Private Collection, Monaco

[p. 16] Exhibition view, *Once upon a Time in City Bild*, Esther Shipper, Cologne, 1990
With Philippe Parreno
Esther Shipper Collection, Berlin

[p. 17] Exhibition view, *French Kiss*, Halle Sud, Geneva, 1990

[p. 18–19] *Try Snaking*, 1991
With Philippe Parreno
Cibachromes, 80 × 60 cm
FRAC Poitou-Charentes Collection, Angoulême

[p. 21] *Paintballer II (Personnage à réactiver)*, 1992
Created at the musée d'Art moderne de la Ville de Paris, Paris, 1992
Cibachrome mounted on aluminum, 120 × 90 cm
Fonds national d'art contemporain Collection, Puteaux

[p. 23] *Catwoman I (Personnage à réactiver)*, 1992
Created for the exhibition *Le Portrait*, musée d'Art moderne et d'Art contemporain, Nice, 1992
Cibachrome mounted on aluminum, 120 × 90 cm
Private Collection, Monaco

[p. 24] *La Belle et la Bête–La Bête (Personnage à réactiver)*, 1993–2011
Reactivation view, *Quand la transgression flirte avec le luxe, Hôtel Particulier*, Paris, 2011
Cibachrome, 60 × 90 cm

[p. 25] *La Belle et la Bête–La Belle (Personnage à réactiver)*, 1992
Created in Édouard Merino's apartment, Monaco
Cibachrome mounted on aluminum, 80 × 120 cm
Julie & Philippe Chiambaretta Collection, Paris

[p. 26] *Guerrier médiéval (Personnage à réactiver)*, 1991
Created for the exhibition *No Man's Time*, Villa Arson, Nice, 1991
Cibachrome, 90 × 60 cm
Christian Zervudacki Collection, Nice

[p. 27] *Art, la Fée (Personnage à réactiver)*, 1992
Created for the exhibition *Maurizio Nannuci*, Villa Arson, Nice, 1992
Cibachrome mounted on aluminum, 60 × 90 cm
Paul-Guy Fournier Collection, Paris

[p. 28] *Le Grand Bleu (Triptyque): La Sorcière (Personnage à réactiver)*, 1993
Created for the exhibition *Cinémas*, Le Quartier, Quimper
Reactivated for the exhibition *Into the Void*, Ikon Gallery, Birmingham, 1996
Cibachrome mounted on PVC, 90 × 60 cm
FRAC Provence-Alpes Côte-d'Azur Collection, Marseille

[p. 29] *Le Policier (Personnage à réactiver)*, 1993
Created for the exhibition *June*, Galerie Thaddaeus Ropac, Paris, 1993
Cibachrome mounted on PVC, 90 × 60 cm
Private Collection, Monaco

[p. 30–31] *Bloody Mary–Virginie, Delphine, Pénélope (Personnages à réactiver)*
With Philippe Perrin

Created for the exhibition *Bloody Mary*, Galerie Jousse Seguin, Paris, 1993
Cibachrome mounted on PVC, 60 × 90 cm

[p. 32] *Catwoman*, "Little Democracy" series, 1997
Installation view, public space, *Boulevard Heurteloup*, Centre de Création Contemporaine, Tours, 1997
Silkscreen on paper, 173.5 × 117 cm
Photographer: Philippe Munda
FRAC Rhône-Alpes Collection, Villeurbanne; Philip Zu Solms von Rödelheim Collection, Germany

[p. 33] *La Répliquante*, "Little Democracy" series, 1997
Installation view, public space, *Boulevard Heurteloup*, Centre de Création Contemporaine, Tours, 1997
Silkscreen on paper, 173.5 × 117 cm
Photographer: Philippe Munda
FRAC Rhône-Alpes Collection, Villeurbanne; Philip Zu Solms von Rödelheim Collection, Germany

[p. 34] *Superman (Personnage à réactiver)*, 1992
Created for the exhibition *Pierre Joseph*, Air de Paris, Nice, 1992
Reactivated for the exhibition *The Living Museum*, Museum für Moderne Kunst, 2003
Decor made with free interpretations of works by Jasper Johns, Hélio Oiticica (as illustrated here), Lucio Fontana, Richard Prince, and Jackson Pollock
Cibachrome, 90 × 60 cm
Philip Zu Solms von Rödelheim Collection, Germany

[p. 36] *Toréador*, "Little Democracy" series, 1997
Installation view, *Boulevard Heurteloup*, Centre de Création Contemporaine, Tours, 1997
Silkscreen on paper, 173.5 × 117 cm
Photographer: Philippe Munda
FRAC Rhône-Alpes Collection, Villeurbanne; Philip Zu Solms von Rödelheim Collection, Germany

[p. 38] *Incrustation Stonewall*, 1997
Blue-screen paint, video editing console, video projection, variable dimensions

[p. 40] *Siberia*, 1988
With Bernard Joisten and Philippe Parreno
Exhibition view, *19&&*, Le Magasin–Centre national d'Art contemporain, Grenoble

[p. 41] *Composit*, 1988
With Bernard Joisten and Philippe Parreno
Exhibition view, *Situation*, Crédac, Ivry-sur-Seine

[p. 42–43] *Jeu des sept erreurs (Cascade)*, 1995
Diptych, digital prints, 42 × 58 cm each
Valéry Grancher Collection, Paris

[p. 44] *Brancusi restauré I*, 1996
Color photograph, 45 × 30 cm
Patrick Perry Collection, Castries

[p. 45] *Voir l'image du côté practicien/Mon cerveau*, 1998, detail
Triptych, silver print mounted on aluminum, 70 × 70 cm

[p. 46–47] *Learning By Experience*, 1998
Exhibition view, Le Consortium, Dijon
Installation, ø 380 cm
FRAC Corse Collection, Corte

[p. 48–49] *Monde érotique*, 1998
Digital print mounted on aluminum, 120 × 180 cm
Cyril Duval Collection, New York; Bruno Serralongue Collection, Paris

[p. 50–51] Exhibition views, *Action Restreinte (Texte de MBK)*, Palais de Tokyo, Paris, 2003
Wall painting, flat screens, Moroso armchair, variable dimensions

[p. 52–53] *Le Livre de la Jungle (Kaa)*, 2005
Exhibition view, Air de Paris, Paris, 2005
Acrylic paint on wall, flat screen, video, 500 × 300 cm

[p. 54–55] *Textes Anaglyphes*, 2007
Exhibition views, *Pierre Joseph*, Forde, Geneva
Francis & Josiane Merino Collection, Monaco

[p. 56–57] *From Apple Core to Glass*, 2010
Exhibition view, *From Apple Core to Glass*, Air de Paris, Paris, 2010
[The materials are classified according to their degree of biodegradability: toilet paper: 2–4 weeks; apple core: 1–5 months; wood: 1–3 years; polystyrene: 50 years; aluminum battery: 200 years; plastic material: 400–450 years; fishing thread and nylon: 600 years; glass: unknown]

[p. 58] *Là, pas là (Table)*, 2010
Exhibition view, *From Apple Core to Glass*, Air de Paris, Paris, 2010
Spray paint, table, chairs, electrical switch, tablecloth, variable dimensions

[p. 59] *Là, pas là (Miroir)*, 2010
Exhibition view, *From Apple Core to Glass*, Air de Paris, Paris, 2010
Spray paint, mirror, variable dimensions
agnès b. Collection, Paris

[p. 60] *Manga (Personnage à réactiver)*, 1997–2007
Created for the exhibition *Images, Objets, Scènes*, Le Magasin–Centre national d'Art contemporain, Grenoble, 1997
Reactivated at Air de Paris, Paris, 2007
Lambda print mounted on aluminum, 120 × 80 cm
Image Division Collection, London

[p. 64] *Football Player (Personnage à réactiver)*, 2012
Created for the Dallas Biennial, Dallas, 2012
Lambda print mounted on aluminum, 120 × 80 cm

Pierre Joseph is represented by Air de Paris, Paris.
www.airdeparis.com

Unless otherwise noted, all works: Courtesy Air de Paris, Paris

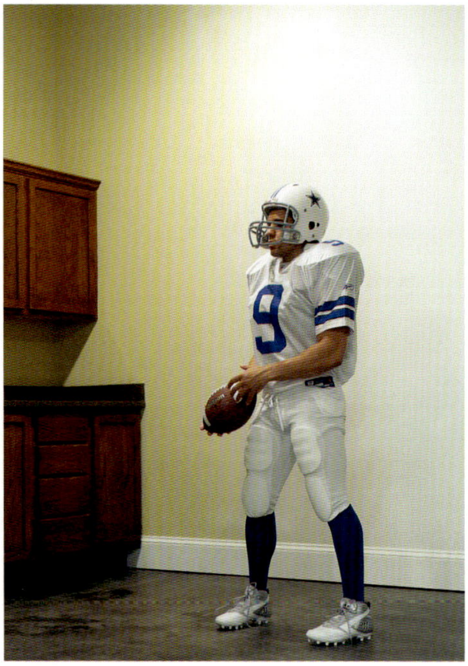

FOOTBALL PLAYER (PERSONNAGE À RÉACTIVER), 2012

EDITORS Lionel Bovier, Clément Dirié
ASSISTANCE Mélanie Borès
AUTHORS Nicolas Bourriaud, Liam Gillick, Stéphanie Moisdon
EDITING AND PROOFREADING Clare Manchester
DESIGN Gavillet & Rust, Geneva
TYPEFACE Hermes (optimo.ch)
PHOTO CREDITS Quentin Bertoux, Pierre Joseph, Eric Troncy, François Fernandez, Marc Domage, Jean-Luc Fournier, André Morin, Daniel Moulinet, Frac Poitou-Charentes, Angoulême/Richard Porteau, Blaise Adilon
COLOR SEPARATION & PRINT Musumeci S.P.A., Quart (Aosta)

The publication had received the support of Image Division Ltd., London, as well as Air de Paris, Paris.

Printed in Europe

Published by
JRP|Ringier
Limmatstrasse 270
CH-8005 Zurich
T +41 (0) 43 311 27 50
F +41 (0) 43 311 27 51
E info@jrp-ringier.com
www.jrp-ringier.com

ISBN: 978-3-03764-285-6

JRP|Ringier books are available internationally at selected bookstores and from the following distribution partners:

Switzerland
AVA Verlagsauslieferung AG
Centralweg 16, CH-8910 Affoltern a.A.
verlagsservice@ava.ch, www.ava.ch

France
Les presses du réel
35 rue Colson, F-21000 Dijon
info@lespressesdureel.com, www.lespressesdureel.com

Germany and Austria
Vice Versa Vertrieb
Immanuelkirchstrasse 12, D-10405 Berlin
info@vice-versa-vertrieb.de, www.vice-versa-vertrieb.de

UK and other European countries
Cornerhouse Publications
70 Oxford Street, UK-Manchester M1 5NH
publications@cornerhouse.org, www.cornerhouse.org/books

USA, Canada, Asia, and Australia
ARTBOOK | D.A.P.
155 Sixth Avenue, 2nd Floor
USA-New York, NY 10013
dap@dapinc.com, www.artbook.com

For a list of our partner bookshops or for any general questions, please contact JRP|Ringier directly at info@ jrp-ringier.com, or visit our homepage www.jrp-ringier.com for further information about our program.

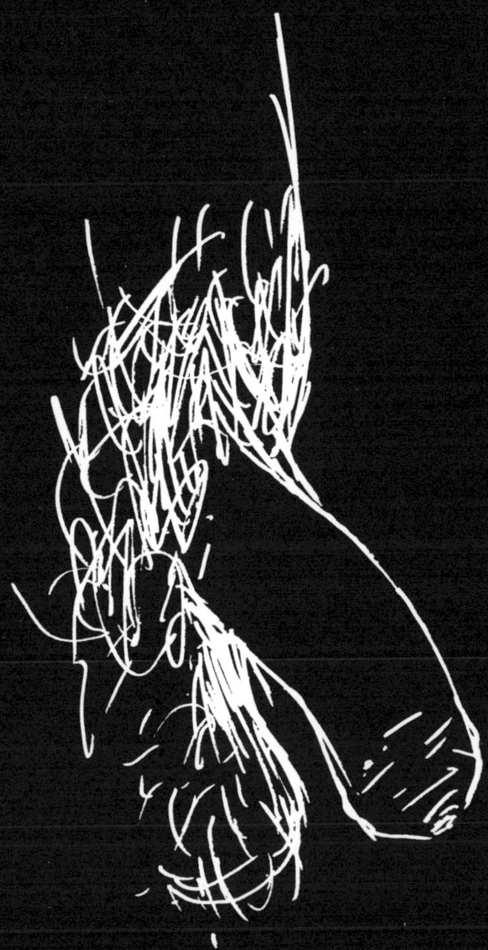